How to Make a California Will

How to Make a California Will

with forms

Kerri de Grosz Stenson
Mark Warda
Attorneys at Law

Sphinx Publishing
A Division of Sourcebooks, Inc.
Naperville, IL • Clearwater, FL

Published by: **Sphinx® Publishing, A Division of Sourcebooks, Inc.®**

Naperville Office
P.O. Box 372
Naperville, Illinois 60566
(630) 961-3900
Fax: 630-961-2168

Clearwater Office
P.O. Box 25
Clearwater, Florida 33757
(813) 587-0999
Fax: 813-586-5088

Interior Design and Production: Shannon E. Harrington, Sourcebooks, Inc.

This publication is designed to provide accurate and authoritative information in regard to the subject matter covered. It is sold with the understanding that the publisher is not engaged in rendering legal, accounting, or other professional service. If legal advice or other expert assistance is required, the services of a competent professional person should be sought.

From a Declaration of Principles Jointly Adopted by a Committee of the American Bar Association and a Committee of Publishers and Associations

Library of Congress Cataloging-in-Publication Data
Stenson, Kerri D.,
How to make a California will : with forms / Kerri D. Stenson, Mark Warda.
p. cm.
Includes index.
ISBN 1-57071-356-1 (pbk.)
1. Wills—California—Popular works. 2. Wills—California—Forms.
I. Warda, Mark. II. Title.
KFC201.Z9S74 1998
346.79405'4—dc21 97-46454
CIP

Printed and bound in the United States of America.

Paperback — 10 9 8 7 6 5 4 3 2 1

CONTENTS

Using Self-Help Law Books

Whenever you shop for a product or service, you are faced with various levels of quality and price. In deciding what product or service to buy, you make a cost/value analysis on the basis of your willingness to pay and the quality you desire.

When buying a car, you decide whether you want transportation, comfort, status, or sex appeal. Accordingly, you decide among such choices as a Neon, a Lincoln, a Rolls Royce, or a Porsche. Before making a decision, you usually weigh the merits of each option against the cost.

When you get a headache, you can take a pain reliever (such as aspirin) or visit a medical specialist for a neurological examination. Given this choice, most people, of course, take a pain reliever, since it costs only pennies, whereas a medical examination costs hundreds of dollars and takes a lot of time. This is usually a logical choice because rarely is anything more than a pain reliever needed for a headache. But in some cases, a headache may indicate something more serious, and failing to see a specialist right away can result in complications. Should everyone with a headache go to a specialist? Of course not, but people treating their own illnesses must realize that they are betting on the basis of their cost/value analysis of the situation, they are taking the most logical option.

The same cost/value analysis must be made in deciding to do one's own legal work. Many legal situations are very straight forward, requiring a simple form and no complicated analysis. Anyone with a little intelligence and a book of instructions can handle the matter without outside help.

But there is always the chance that complications are involved that only an attorney would notice. To simplify the law into a book like this, several legal cases often must be condensed into a single sentence or paragraph. Otherwise, the book would be several hundred pages long and too complicated for most people. However, this simplification necessarily leaves out many details and nuances that would apply to special or unusual situations. Also, there are many ways to interpret most legal questions. Your case may come before a judge who disagrees with the analysis of our authors.

Therefore, in deciding to use a self-help law book and to do your own legal work, you must realize that you are making a cost/value analysis and deciding that the chance your case will not turn out to your satisfaction is outweighed by the money you will save in doing it yourself. Most people handling their own simple legal matters never have a problem, but occasionally people find that it ended up costing them more to have an attorney straighten out the situation than it would have if they had hired an attorney in the beginning. Keep this in mind while handling your case, and be sure to consult an attorney if you feel you might need further guidance.

Introduction

This book was written to help you, as a California resident, quickly and easily make your own will without the expense or delay of hiring a lawyer. It begins with a short explanation of how a will works and what a will can and cannot do. It is designed to allow those with simple estates to quickly and inexpensively set up their affairs to distribute their property according to their wishes. It includes an explanation of how such things as joint property and "pay on death" accounts will affect your planning.

It also includes information on appointing a guardian for any minor children you may have. This can be useful in avoiding bad feelings between relatives and in protecting the children from being raised by someone you would object to.

Chapters 1 through 7 explain the laws that affect the making of a will. Appendix A is a glossary of terms that you may encounter in this book, in any other research you may do, in discussing wills with a lawyer, or in some other context. Appendix B contains sample filled-in will forms to show you how it is done. Appendix C contains blank will forms you can use.

You can prepare your own will quickly and easily by using the forms out of the book, or by photocopying them, or you can retype the material on sheets of paper. The small amount of time it takes to do this can give you and your loved ones the peace of mind of knowing that your estate will be distributed according to your wishes.

A surprising number of people have had their estates pass to the wrong parties because of a simple lack of knowledge of how the laws work. Before using any of the forms in appendix C, you should read and understand all of the previous chapters of this book.

In each example given in the text you might ask, "What if the spouse died first?" or "What if the children were grown up?" and then the answer might be different. If your situation is at all complicated, you are advised to seek the advice of an attorney. In many communities, wills are available for very reasonable prices. No book of this type can cover every contingency in every case, but a knowledge of the basics will help you to make the right decisions regarding your property.

The forms in this book are for simple wills to leave property to your family, or if you have no family, to friends or charities. As explained in chapter 2, if you wish to disinherit your family and leave your property to others you should consult with an attorney who can be sure that your will cannot be successfully challenged in court.

1 Basic Rules You Should Know

Before making your will, you should understand how a will works and what it can and cannot do. Otherwise, your plans may not be carried out and the wrong people may end up with your property.

What Is a Will?

A will is a document you can use to control who gets your property, who will be guardian of your children and their property, and who will manage your estate upon your death.

How a Will Is Used

Some people think a will avoids probate. It does not. A will is the document used in probate to determine who receives what property, who is appointed guardian of any minor children, and who is appointed executor or personal representative of your estate.

Avoiding Probate

If you wish to avoid probate you need to use methods other than a will, such as joint ownership, pay-on-death accounts, or living trusts. The first two of these are discussed later in this chapter. For information on living trusts you should refer to a book which focuses on trusts as used for estate planning. *Living Trusts and Simple Ways to Avoid Probate* is available from your local bookstores, or directly from the publisher of this book.

If a person successfully avoids probate with all of his or her property, then he or she may not need a will. In most cases, when a husband or wife dies, no will or probate is necessary because everything is owned jointly. However, everyone should have a will in case some property, that one forgot to put into joint ownership or that was received just prior to death, does not avoid probate for some reason, or if both husband and wife die in the same accident.

JOINT TENANCY AVOIDS PROBATE

Property that is owned in *joint tenancy with right of survivorship* does not pass under a will. If a will gives property to one person, but that property is already in a joint account with another person, the will is usually ignored and the joint owner of the account gets the property. This is because the property in the account avoids probate and passes directly to the joint owner. A will only controls property that goes through probate. There are exceptions to this rule. If money is put into a joint account only for convenience, it might pass under the will; but if the joint owner does not give it up, it could take an expensive court battle to get it back.

Putting property into joint tenancy does not give absolute rights to it. If the estate owes estate taxes, the recipient of joint tenancy property may have to contribute to the tax payment.

EXAMPLES

☛ Ted and his wife want all of their property to go to the survivor of them. They put their house, cars, bank accounts, and brokerage accounts in joint ownership. When Ted dies, his wife only has to show his death certificate to get all the property transferred to her name. No probate or will is necessary.

- After Ted's death, his wife, Michelle puts all of the property and accounts into joint ownership with her son, Mark. Upon her death, Mark needs only to present her death certificate to have everything transferred into his name. No probate or will is necessary.

Joint Tenancy Overrules Your Will

If all property is in joint ownership or if all property is distributed through a will, things are simple. But when some property passes by each method, a person's plans may not be fulfilled.

Examples

- Bill's will leaves all his property to his sister, Mary. Bill dies owning a house jointly with his wife, Joan, and a bank account jointly with his son, Don. Upon Bill's death Joan gets the house, Don gets the bank account and his sister, Mary, gets nothing.
- Betty's will leaves half her assets to Ann and half her assets to George. Betty dies owning $1,000,000 in stock jointly with George, and a car in her name alone. Ann gets only a half interest in the car. George gets all the stock and a half interest in the car.
- John's will leaves all his property equally to his five children. Before going in the hospital he puts his oldest son, Harry, as a joint owner of his accounts. John dies and Harry gets all of his assets. The rest of the children get nothing.

In each of these cases the property went to a person it probably shouldn't have because the decedent didn't realize that joint ownership overruled his or her will. In some families this might not be a problem. In the third example, Harry might divide the property equally (and possibly pay a gift tax). But in many cases, Harry would just keep everything and the family would take nothing despite John's will.

Joint Tenancy Can Be Risky

In many cases joint tenancy can be an ideal way to own property and avoid probate. However it does have risks. If you put your real estate in joint ownership with someone, you cannot sell it or mortgage it without that person's signature. If you put your bank account in joint ownership with someone, they can draw money out of the account.

Examples

- Alice put her house in joint ownership with her son. She later married Ed and moved in with him. She wanted to sell her house and to invest the money for income. Her son refused to sign the deed because he wanted to keep the home in the family. She was in court for ten months getting her house back and the judge almost refused to do it.

- Alex put his bank accounts into joint ownership with his daughter Mary to avoid probate. Mary fell in love with Doug who was in trouble with the law. Doug talked Mary into "borrowing" $30,000 from the account for a "business deal" that went sour. Later she "borrowed" $25,000 more to pay Doug's bail bond. When Alex later sought to withdraw some money from the account, he discovered that his money was gone.

Tenancy in Common Does Not Avoid Probate

In California, there are three basic ways to own property: joint tenancy with right of survivorship, tenancy in common, and tenancy by the entirety. *Joint tenancy with right of survivorship* means that if one owner of the property dies, the survivor automatically gets the decedent's share. *Tenancy in common* means when one owner dies, that owner's share of the property goes to his or her heirs or beneficiaries under the will. *Tenancy by the entirety* is like joint tenancy with right of survivorship, but it can only apply to a married couple.

EXAMPLES

- Tom and Marcia bought a house and lived together for twenty years. The deed did not specify joint tenancy. When Tom died his brother inherited his half of the house. If Marcia could not afford to buy the other half of the house from Tom's brother, the house would have to be sold.

- Lindsay and her husband Rocky bought a house. When Rocky suddenly died, Lindsay obtained full ownership of the house by filing a death certificate at the courthouse. The deed to the house stated that they were husband and wife, therefore, ownership was presumed to be tenancy by the entirety.

A Spouse Can Overrule a Will

California is a *community property* state. Under community property law, all property acquired during the marriage by the labor of either spouse is considered community property and a surviving spouse is entitled to fifty percent of the community property. Under community property laws it is more important how and when property was acquired than whose name is on the title..

EXAMPLES

- John's will leaves all of his property to his children of a prior marriage and nothing to his wife who is already wealthy. John's wife gets fifty percent of the community property. The children divide the remainder of John's estate.

- Mary puts half of her property in a joint account with her husband, and in her will she leaves all of her separate property to her sister who is ill. When Mary dies, her husband gets all of the money in the joint account and fifty percent of the community property. Mary's sister takes the remainder of the estate.

A Spouse's Share Can Be Avoided

While some feel it is wrong to avoid giving a spouse the share allowed by law, there are legitimate reasons for doing so (such as where there are children from a prior marriage) and the law allows exceptions.

The easiest way to avoid an assumption of community property is for your spouse to sign a written agreement either before or after the marriage. While many spouses express the greatest fondness for their stepchildren, getting them to sign over a large share of his or her estate can be a challenge.

Other ways to avoid a presumption of community property are to have all property in joint ownership with others, or in trust.

EXAMPLE

☛ Dan owns his stocks jointly with his son. He owns his bank accounts jointly with his daughter. If he owned this property prior to his marriage it is his separate property and may pass to his children by right of survivorship.

Another way to leave something to someone other than your spouse and avoid having it called community property is to obtain a life insurance policy naming someone other than your spouse as beneficiary.

Avoiding a spouse's share, especially without his or her knowledge, opens the possibility of a lawsuit after your death, and if your actions were not done to precise legal requirements they could be thrown out. Therefore, you should consider consulting an attorney if you plan to leave your spouse less than the share provided by law.

I/T/F Bank Accounts Are Better Than Joint Ownership

One way to keep bank accounts out of your estate and still retain control is to title them *in trust for,* or I/T/F, with a named a beneficiary.

Some banks may use the letters POD for *pay on death* or TOD for *transfer on death*. Either way the result is the same. No one except you can get the money until your death, and on death it immediately goes directly to the person you name, without a will or probate proceeding. These are sometimes called *Totten Trusts* after the court case that declared them legal.

EXAMPLE ☛ Rich opened a bank account in the name of "Rich, In Trust For Mary." If Rich dies, the money automatically goes to Mary, but prior to his death Mary has no control over the account, doesn't even have to know about it, and Rich can take Mary's name off the account at any time.

There Are Special Rules for Homesteads

A *homestead* for estate purposes, often referred to as a *probate homestead,* is property that is the permanent residence of a legal resident of California who has a spouse or minor children, and who owns the property in his or her name alone. Homestead laws generally declare such family home to be the property of the surviving spouse and minor children, free of the claims of creditors.

If your personal property is homestead, your will has no control over it. Upon your death, your homestead automatically passes as follows:

1. If you have both a spouse and minor children, your spouse gets the right to live in the homestead for the rest of his or her life, and your children get it upon your spouse's death.
2. If you have a spouse and no minor children, your spouse gets the homestead, no matter what your will says.
3. If you have minor children, but no spouse, your children get the homestead in equal shares, no matter what your will says.

There is an exception: If you have a spouse and *adult* children, you can will the homestead to your spouse.

Whether or not a home is legally homestead can be a tricky legal question. It may depend on which spouse is providing the support, or whether the property is also being used for business purposes. If you have a question as to whether your property is a homestead for estate purposes, you should consult a lawyer who is experienced in estate planning.

Because homestead property can only be property that is in individual ownership, jointly held property and property in trust does not come under these rules. To avoid property becoming homestead property, it must be purchased in joint names or in trust. If it is already in an individual's name, it must be put in trust or in joint ownership without the spouse's signature.

It is possible to set up the title to your home in such a way that it will not be homestead and your spouse cannot claim an interest in it (for example, if you want it to go to your children from a previous marriage). However, this should be done by a lawyer who is familiar with the latest cases in this area. If it is done wrong, it may be thrown out by a court. In such a situation you should also consider a written agreement with your spouse regarding the home.

Some Property May Be Exempt from Your Will

If you have a spouse or minor children, the court may set apart tangible personal property that is regularly used by you or members of your family, as exempt from your will. This property would include such items as household furnishings, appliances, and other personal effects, and is called *exempt property*. If you have a spouse, your spouse gets this property. If you do not have a spouse, your children get it. Additionally, a spouse or minor children may get a *family allowance*, the amount of which may be determined by the court.

To avoid having property declared exempt, it may be *specifically* given to someone in a will. If certain items are specifically given to certain persons, those items will not be considered part of the exempt property. Cash kept in a joint or I/T/F bank account would go to the joint owner or beneficiary and not be used as the family allowance.

Getting Married Automatically Changes Your Will

If you get married after making your will and do not rewrite it after the wedding, your spouse gets a share of your estate as if you had no will, unless you have a pre-marital agreement, or you made a provision for your spouse in the will, or you stated specifically in the will that you intended not to mention your prospective spouse.

EXAMPLE

☛ John made his will leaving everything to his brother. When he married Joan, an heiress with plenty of money, he didn't change his will because he still wanted his brother to get his estate. When he died, Joan got 100% of the community property and 50% of John's separate property. John's brother received the remainder of his separate property.

Getting Divorced Automatically Changes Your Will

In some states, getting divorced automatically deletes your former spouse's share from your will. However, you should not rely on this, and you should make a new will. If your spouse tries to get a share of the estate because he or she is mentioned, it may cost your estate considerable legal fees to defeat the claim.

EXAMPLE ☛ George and Eunice made their wills leaving half their property to each other and half to their children from their previous marriages. After their divorce, George forgot to make a new will. When George died, Eunice hired a lawyer to file papers claiming half the estate. His children's lawyer pointed out that her share was void because of the divorce, but the other lawyer demanded a trial, hoping the children would settle the case by giving his client a few thousand dollars. They refused to settle but their attorney charged $5,000 for the trial.

In some states divorce does *not* revoke your will. If you do not have time to make a new will after your divorce, you may want to revoke your will. This can be done by tearing it up or by other ways discussed in chapter 5. By revoking your will you are choosing to use your state's distribution system of deciding your heirs, which in all cases would not include your ex-spouse. See chapter 2.

Having Children Automatically Changes Your Will

If you have a child after making your will and do not rewrite it, the child gets a share of your estate as if there was no will.

EXAMPLE ☛ Dave made a will leaving half his estate to his sister and the other half to his three children. He later had another child and didn't revise his will. In some states, upon his death his fourth child would get one quarter of his estate, his sister would get three-eighths and the other three children would each get one-eighth.

It is best to rewrite your will at the birth of a child. However, another solution is to include the following clause after the names of your children in your will.

```
"...and any afterborn children living at the
time of my death, in equal shares."
```

How Your Debts Are Paid

One of the duties of the person administering an estate is to pay the debts of the decedent. Before an estate is distributed the legitimate debts must be ascertained and paid.

An exception is *secured debts,* these are debts that are protected by a lien against property, like a home loan or a car loan. In the case of a secured debt, the loan does not have to be paid before the property is distributed.

EXAMPLE ☛ John owns a $100,000 house with a $80,000 mortgage and he has $100,000 in the bank. If he leaves the house to his brother and the bank account to his sister then his brother would get the home but would owe the $80,000 mortgage.

What if your debts are more than your property? Today, unlike hundreds of years ago, people cannot inherit other peoples' debts. A person's property is used to pay their probate and funeral expenses first, and if there is not enough left to pay their other debts, then the creditors are out of luck. However, if a person leaves property to people and does not have enough assets to pay his or her debts, then the property will be sold to pay the debts.

EXAMPLE ☛ Jeb's will leaves all of his property to his three children. At the time of his death, Jeb, has $30,000 in medical bills, $11,000 in credit card debt, and his only assets are his car and $5,000 in stock. The car and stock would be sold and the funeral bill and probate fees paid out of the proceeds. If any money was left it would go to the creditors and nothing would be left for the children. The children would not have to pay the medical bills or credit card debt.

Estate and Inheritance Taxes

Unlike some states, California does not have estate or inheritance taxes in most cases. The only time estate taxes would be paid to the state of California would be if the estate was subject to federal estate taxes and a credit was allowed for state taxes. Then these taxes would be paid to the state and credited against the federal tax due.

There is a federal estate tax for estates above the amount of the *unified credit*. The unified credit is the amount a person can leave at death or through gifts during his or her lifetime. In 1998, this amount is $625,000 but it will rise to $1,000,000 by the year 2006. The amount will change according to the following schedule.

Year	**Amount**
1998	$625,000
1999	$650,000
2000-2001	$675,000
2002-2003	$700,000
2004	$850,000
2005	$950,000
2006	$1,000,000

Annual Exclusion

When a person makes a gift, that gift is subtracted from the unified credit available to his or her estate at death. However, a person is allowed to make gifts of up to $10,000 per person per year without having these subtracted from the unified credit. This means a married couple can make gifts of up to $20,000 per person. The Taxpayer Relief Act of 1997 provided that this exclusion amount will be adjusted for inflation.

Do You Need a California Will? 2

What a Will Can Do

Beneficiaries

A will allows you to decide who gets your property after your death. You can give specific personal items to certain persons and choose which of your friends or relatives, if any, deserve a greater share of your estate. You can also leave gifts to schools and charities.

Personal Representative

A will allows you to decide who will be the *personal representative* of your estate. This is the person who gathers together all your assets and distributes them to the beneficiaries, hires attorneys or accountants if necessary, and files any essential tax or probate forms. In some states, this person may be called the *executor*, or *administrator*. With a will, you can provide that your personal representative does not have to post a surety bond with the court in order to serve and this can save your estate some money. You can also give the personal representative the power to sell your property and take other actions without getting a court order.

Guardian

A will allows you to choose a guardian for your minor children. This way you can avoid fights among relatives and make sure the best person raises your children. You may also appoint separate guardians over your children and over their money. For example you may appoint your sister as guardian over your children, and your father as guardian over their money. That way, a second person can keep an eye on how the children's money is being spent.

PROTECTING HEIRS

You can set up a trust to provide that your property is not distributed immediately. Many people feel that their children would not be ready to handle large sums of money at the age of majority, which in most states is eighteen. A will can direct that the money is held until the children are twenty-one, or twenty-five, or older.

MINIMIZING TAXES

If your estate is over $625,000 (this amount will rise to $1,000,000 over the next ten years) then it will be subject to federal estate taxes. If you wish to lower those taxes, for example by making gifts to charities, you can do so through a will. However, such estate planning is beyond the scope of this book and you should consult an estate planning attorney or another book for further information.

What If You Do Not Have a Will?

If you do not have a will, California law says that your property will be distributed as follows:

- All of your *community property* passes to your spouse.
- Your *separate property* passes as follows:
  - If you leave a spouse your spouse receives the following share:
    - if you leave no children, parents, siblings, nieces or nephews, then your spouse receives all of your property.
    - if you leave one child, or one or more parents, siblings, nieces or nephews, your spouse receives one-half of your separate property.
    - if you leave two or more children, your spouse receives one-third of your separate property.

- The share that does not pass to your spouse, or if you do not leave a spouse, passes as follows.
    1. Your children.
    2. Your parents.
    3. Your brothers and sisters, or if they are dead, their children.
    4. Your grandparents, or if they are dead, their children (i.e., your uncles and aunts).
    5. Children of your deceased spouse.
    6. Relatives of your deceased spouse.
    7. The State of California.

Note: In the above examples, where a child is deceased any children of that child would take the child's share.

Is Your Out-of-State Will Valid in California?

A will that is valid in another state would probably be valid to pass property in California. However, if your will is not *self-proved,* under the law of the state in which it was signed or under California law, it could not be accepted by a California Probate Court until the witnesses have signed an oath that they saw you sign the will. A person in your former state would have to be appointed as a *commissioner* to take the oath of a person who witnessed your signature on the will. Because of the expense and delay in having a commissioner appointed, and the problems in finding out-of-state witnesses, it is advisable to execute a new will after moving to California.

California allows a will to be self-proved, so that the witnesses never have to be called in to take an oath or give testimony. With special self-proving language in your will, the witnesses take the oath at the time of signing.

Who Can Make a California Will?

In California, any person who is at least eighteen years of age and of sound mind may make a will.

What a Will Cannot Do

A will cannot direct that anything illegal be done and it cannot put unreasonable conditions on a gift. For example, a provision that your daughter gets all of your property if she divorces her husband would be ignored by the court. She would get the property with no conditions attached. You can put some conditions in your will, but to be sure they are enforceable you should consult with an attorney.

A will cannot leave money or property to an animal because animals cannot legally own property. If you wish to continue paying for care of an animal after your death, you should leave the funds in trust or to a friend whom you know will care for the animal.

Who Can Use a Simple Will?

The wills in this book will pass your property whether your estate is $1,000 or $100,000,000. However, if your estate is over $625,000 (this amount will rise to $1,000,000 over the next ten years) then you might be able to avoid estate taxes by using a trust or other tax-saving device. The larger your estate, the more you can save on estate taxes by doing more complicated planning. If you have a large estate and are concerned about estate taxes, you should consult an estate planning attorney or a book on estate planning.

Who Should Not Use a Simple Will?

Will Contest If you expect that there may be a fight over your estate or that someone might contest your will's validity, you should consult a lawyer. If you leave less than the statutory share of your estate to your spouse or if you leave one or more of your children out of your will, it is likely that someone will contest your will.

Complex Estates If you are the beneficiary of a trust or have any complications in your legal relationships, you may need special provisions in your will.

Blind or Unable to Write A person who is blind or who can sign only with an "X" should also consult a lawyer about the proper way to make and execute a will.

Estates Over $625,000 If you expect to have over $625,000 (this amount will rise to $1,000,000 over the next ten years) at the time of your death, you may want to consult with a CPA or tax attorney regarding tax consequences.

Conditions If you wish to put some sort of conditions or restrictions on the property you leave, you should consult a lawyer. For example, if you want to leave money to your brother only if he quits smoking, or to a hospital only if they name a wing in your honor, you should consult an attorney to be sure that your conditions are valid in your state.

How to Make a Simple Will 3

Identifying Parties in Your Will

PEOPLE

When making your will, it is important to clearly identify the persons you name as your beneficiaries. In some families, names differ only by middle initial or by Jr. or Sr. Be sure to check everyone's name before making your will. You can also add your relationship to the beneficiary, and their location such as "my cousin, George Smith, of Petaluma, California."

ORGANIZATIONS

The same applies to organizations and charities. For example there is more than one group using the words "cancer society" or "heart association" in their name. Be sure to get the correct name of the group to which you intend to leave your gift.

Specific Bequests

Occasionally a person will want to leave a little something to a friend or charity, and the rest to the family. This can be done with a *specific bequest* such as "$1,000 to my dear friend Martha Jones." Of course there could be a problem if, at the time of a person's death, there wasn't anything left after the specific bequests.

EXAMPLE ☛ At the time of making his will, Todd had $1,000,000 in assets. He felt generous so he left $50,000 to a local hospital, $50,000 to a local group that took care of homeless animals and the rest to his children. Unfortunately, several years later, the stock market crashed and he committed suicide by jumping off a bridge. His estate at the time was worth only $110,000 so after the above specific bequests and the legal fees and expenses of probate, there was nothing left for his five children.

Another problem with specific bequests is that some of the property may be worth considerably more or less at death than when the will was made.

EXAMPLE ☛ Joe wanted his two children to equally share his estate. His will left his son his stocks (worth $500,000 at the time) and his daughter $500,000 in cash. By the time of Joe's death the stock was only worth $100,000.

He should have left "fifty percent" of his estate to each child. If giving certain things to certain people is an important part of your estate plan, you can give specific items to specific persons, but remember to make changes if your assets change.

JOINT BENEFICIARIES

Be careful about leaving one item of personal property to more than one person. For example, if you leave something to your son and his wife, what would happen if they divorce? Even if you leave something to two of your own children, what if they can't agree about who will have possession of it? Whenever possible, leave property to one person.

REMAINDER CLAUSE

One of the most important clauses in a will is the *remainder clause*. This is the clause that says something like "all the rest of my property I leave to..." This clause makes sure that the will disposes of all property owned at the time of death and that nothing is forgotten.

In a simple will the best way to distribute property is to put it all in the remainder clause. In the first example in the previous section, the problem would have been avoided if the will had read as follows: "The rest, residue, and remainder of my estate I leave, five percent to ABC Hospital, five percent to XYZ Animal Welfare League, and ninety percent to be divided equally among my children..."

Alternate Beneficiaries

You should always provide for an *alternate beneficiary* in case the first one dies before you and you do not have a chance to make out a new will.

Survivor or Descendants

Suppose your will leaves your property to your sister and brother, but your brother dies before you. Should his share go to your sister or to your brother's children or grandchildren?

If you are giving property to two or more persons, and if you want it all to go to the other if one of them dies, then you would specify "or the survivor of them."

If, on the other hand, you want the property to go to the children of the deceased person you should state in your will, "or their lineal descendants." This would include his or her children and grandchildren.

Family or Person

If you decide you want it to go to your brother's children and grandchildren, you must next decide if an equal share should go to each family or to each person. For example, if your brother leaves three grandchildren, and one is an only child of his daughter and the others are the children of his son, should all grandchildren get equal shares, or should they take their parent's share?

When you want each family to get an equal share it is called *per stirpes*. When you want each person to get an equal share it is called *per capita*. Most of the wills in this book use per stirpes because that is the most common way property is left. If you wish to leave your property per capita then you can rewrite the will with this change.

EXAMPLE ☛ Alice leaves her property to her two daughters, Mary and Pat in equal shares, or to their lineal descendants per stirpes. Both daughters die before Alice. Mary leaves one child; Pat leaves two children. In this case Mary's child would get half of the estate and Pat's children would split the other half of the estate. If Alice had specified per capita instead of per stirpes then each child would have gotten one-third of the estate.

Per Stirpes Distribution

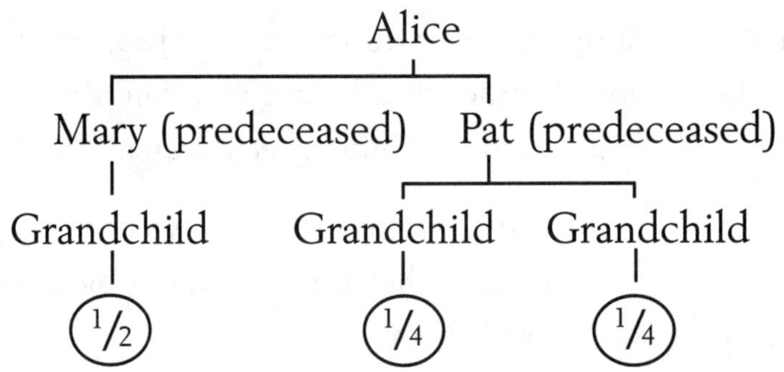

Per Capita Distribution

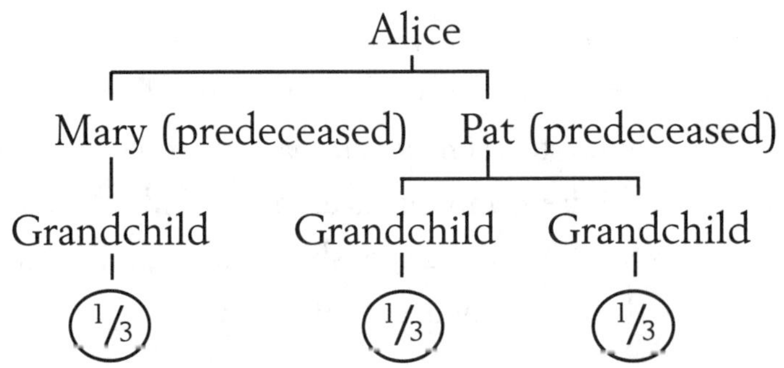

There are fourteen different will forms in this book that should cover the options most people want, but you may want to divide your property slightly differently from what is stated in these forms. If so, you can retype the forms according to these rules, specifying whether the property should go to the survivor or the lineal descendants. If this is confusing to you, you should consider seeking the advice of an attorney.

SURVIVORSHIP

Many people put a clause in their will stating that anyone receiving property under the will must survive for thirty days (or forty-five or sixty) after the death of the person who made the will. This is so that if the two people die in the same accident there will not be two probates and the property will not go to the other party's heirs. In any case, under California law, a person must survive you by 120 hours in order to take a gift under the will.

EXAMPLE ☛ Fred and Wilma were married and each had children by previous marriages. They didn't have survivorship clauses in their wills and they were in an automobile crash. Wilma died instantly, but Fred was in the hospital for a week before he died. When Wilma died, all of her property went to Fred. When Fred died, all of Fred *and* Wilma's property went to his children. Wilma's children got nothing.

GUARDIANS

If you have minor children you should name a guardian for them. There are two types of guardians, a guardian over the *person* and a guardian over the *property*. The first is the person who decides where the children will live and makes the other parental decisions for them. A guardian of the property is in charge of the minor's property and inheritance. In most cases, one person is appointed guardian of both the person and property. But some people prefer the children to live with one person, but to have the money held by another person.

EXAMPLE ☛ Sandra was a widow with a young daughter. She knew that if anything happened to her, her sister would be the best person to raise her daughter. But her sister was never good with money. So when Sandra made out her will, she named her sister as guardian over the person of her daughter and she named her father as guardian over the estate of her daughter.

When naming a guardian, it is always advisable to name an alternate guardian in case your first choice is unable to serve for any reason.

CHILDREN'S TRUST

When a parent dies leaving a minor child and the child's property is held by a guardian, the guardianship ends when the child reaches the age of eighteen, and all of the property is turned over to the child. Most parents do not feel their children are competent at the age of eighteen to handle large sums of money, and prefer that it be held until the child is twenty-one, twenty-five, thirty, or even older.

If you wish to set up a complicated system of determining when your children should receive various amounts of your estate, or if you want the property held to a higher age than thirty-five, you should consult a lawyer to draft a trust. However, if you want a simple provision that the funds be held until they reach a higher age than eighteen, and you have someone you trust to make decisions about paying for education or other expenses for your child or children, you can put that provision in your will as a childrens' trust.

The childrens' trust trustee can be the same person as the guardian or a different person. It is advisable to name an alternate trustee if your first choice is unable to handle it.

Statutory Wills

A *statutory* will is a will which complies with California Probate Code §6240. This law states that if a will contains certain language and is witnessed by two persons it can be admitted to probate without further documentation or proceedings.

Handwritten Wills

In California, a will that is entirely handwritten (called a *holographic* will) is also valid, even if there are no witnesses, but the material provisions of the will and the signature must be in your own handwriting. Since there is a greater chance a holographic will may be held invalid for some reason, it will should only be used if you are in an emergency situation and are unable to find two persons to sign as witnesses.

Witnesses

As explained above, a California statutory will must be witnessed by two persons to be valid but a handwritten will does not.

Notary

In California, neither a statutory will nor a handwritten will needs to be notarized.

Self-Proving Affidavit

In most states a *self-proving* affidavit can be added to a will which will allow the will to be admitted to probate without further documentation. In California this affidavit is unnecessary as long as the right language is included in the will and it is witnessed by two persons.

Personal Representative

A *personal representative* (also called an *executor* or *administrator*) is the person who will be in charge of your probate. He or she will gather your assets, handle the sale of them if necessary, prepare an inventory, hire an attorney, and distribute the property. This should be a person you trust, and if it is, then you can state in your will that no bond will be required to be posted by him or her. Otherwise the court will require that a surety bond be paid for by your estate to guaranty that the person is honest. You can appoint a bank to handle your estate but their fees are usually very high.

It is best to appoint a California resident as personal representative, both because it is easier and because a bond may be required of a non-resident even if your will waives a bond.

Some people like to name two persons as personal representative to avoid jealousy, or to have them check on each other's honesty. However, this is not a good idea. It makes double work in getting the papers signed, and there can be problems if they cannot agree on something.

The personal representative is entitled to some compensation for his or her services to the estate. You may specify a fee in your will, but if you do not, the court will use a percentage formula starting with four percent on the first $15,000 and decreasing to a fraction of a percent on multi-million dollar estates. A family member will often waive the fee, but if there is a lot of work involved he or she may request the fee, or other family members may insist that he or she take one. You can insist in your will that your executor/personal representative is paid a fee.

Unless such power is given in a will a personal representative cannot sell real estate without approval by the court. If you trust your executor you can avoid the expense and delay of this by giving him or her the power to do so without court approval.

Disinheriting Someone

Because it may result in your will being challenged in court, you should not make your own will if you intend to disinherit someone. However, you may wish to leave one child less than another because you already made a gift to that child, or perhaps that child needs the money less than the other.

If you do give more to one child than to another, then you should state your reasons to show that you thought out your plan. Otherwise the one who received less might argue that you didn't realize what you were doing and were not competent to make a will.

Funeral Arrangements

There is no harm in stating your preferences in your will, but directions for a funeral are not legally enforceable. Often a will is not found until after the funeral. Therefore, it is better to tell your family about your wishes or to make prior arrangements yourself.

Forms

There are several different forms included in this book for easy use. You can either cut them out or photocopy them, or you can retype them on plain paper.

The forms in this book are printed on both sides of the page. If you photocopy them on separate pages or type your will on more than one piece of paper you should staple the pages together, initial each page and have both witnesses initial each page and each page should state at the bottom, "page 1 of 3," "page 2 of 3," etc.

Corrections

Your will should have no white-outs or erasures. If for some reason it is impossible to make a will without corrections, they should be initialed by you and both witnesses.

4 How to Execute Your Will

The signing of a will is a serious legal event and must be done properly or the will may be declared invalid. Preferably, it should be done in a private room without distraction. The witnesses should watch each other sign and no one should leave the scene until all have signed.

EXAMPLE

- Ebenezer was bedridden in a small room. His will was brought in to him to sign. The witnesses then came into the room and signed the will. Ebenezer never acknowledged his signature to the witnesses. Ebenezer's will was ignored by the court and his property went to two persons who were not in his will.

PROCEDURE

To be sure your will is valid, you should follow these rules:

- You must date your will and sign your name at the end, in ink, exactly as it is printed in the will, and you should initial each page. You must either sign the will or acknowledge your signature in the presence of two witnesses who are present at the same time.
- The witnesses must each sign the will.

COPIES

It is a good idea to make at least one copy of your will, but you should not personally sign the copies or have them notarized. The reasons for this are:

1. If you later cancel or destroy your will, someone may produce a copy and have it probated.

2. If you lose or destroy a copy of your will, a court may assume you intended to revoke the original.

EXAMPLE ☛ Michael typed out a copy of his will and made two photocopies. He had the original and both copies signed and notarized. He then gave the original to his sister who was his executor and kept the two copies. Upon his death the two copies were not found among his papers. Because these copies were in his possession and not found it was assumed that he destroyed them. A court ruled that by destroying them he must have intended to revoke the original will and his property went to persons not listed in his will.

5 After You Sign Your Will

Storing Your Will

Your will should be kept in a place safe from fire and easily accessible to your heirs. Your personal representative should know of its whereabouts. It can be kept in a home safe or fire box.

In some states the opening of a safe deposit box in a bank after a person's death is a complicated affair, but in California it is easy to get a will out of a deceased person's safe deposit box.

If you are close to your children and can trust them explicitly, then you could allow one of them to keep the will in his or her safe deposit box. However, if you later decide to limit that child's share there could be a problem.

Example ☛ Diane made out her will giving her property to her two children equally, and she gave the will to her older child, Bill, to hold. Years later, Bill moved away and her younger child, Mary, took care of her by coming over every day. Diane made a new will giving most of her property to Mary. Upon Diane's death Bill came to town and found the new will in Diane's house, but he destroyed it and probated the old will which gave him half the property.

Wills are not filed anywhere until after a person's death. No one has to know what you have put in your will while you are alive. An attorney preparing a will might offer to keep it in his safe deposit box at no charge. This way, he or she will likely be contacted at the time of death, and will be in a good position to do the lucrative probate work.

Revoking Your Will

The usual way to revoke a will is to execute a new one that states that it revokes all previously made wills. To revoke a will without making a new one, one can tear, burn, cancel, deface, obliterate, or destroy it, as long as this is done with the intention of revoking it. If this is done accidentally, then the will is not legally revoked.

Example

☛ Ralph tells his son Clyde to go to the basement safe and tear up his (Ralph's) will. If Clyde does not tear it up in Ralph's presence it is probably not effectively revoked.

Revival of Previous Will

What if you change your will by drafting a new one and later decide you don't like the changes and want to go back to your old will? Can you destroy the new one and revive the old one? NO! Once you execute a new will revoking an old will, you cannot revive the old will unless you execute a new document stating that you intend to revive the old will. In other words, you really should execute a new will.

Changing Your Will

You should not make any changes on a witnessed will after it has been signed, however, you may make handwritten changes to a handwritten will (also called a *holographic will*). If you cross out a person's name or add a clause to a will that has already been signed, your change will not be valid and your entire will might become invalid.

One way to amend a witnessed will is to execute a *codicil.* A codicil is an amendment to a will. However, a codicil must be executed just like a will and must have two witnesses. Because a codicil requires the same formality as a will, it is usually better to just make a new will.

To prepare a codicil, use Form 17.

6 How to Make a Living Will

No, a *living will* is not a videotape of a person making a will. It has nothing to do with the usual type of will that distributes property. A living will is a document by which a person declares that he or she does not want artificial life support systems used if he or she becomes terminally ill.

Modern science can often keep a body alive, even if the brain is permanently dead or if the person is in constant pain. In 1976, California passed a law that allowed a living will for the first time. Under this law, a living will can be signed at any time. It must be signed in front of two witnesses, and at least one of the witnesses may not be entitled to any portion of the patient's estate. In addition, a health care provider, the operator of a community care facility, the operator of a residential care facility for the elderly or any employee thereof may not be a witness. If the person is physically unable to sign, he or she may read the living will out loud and direct one of the witnesses to sign it for him or her.

A living will form is included in appendix C of this book.

7 How to Make Anatomical Gifts

Since 1970, California has allowed its residents to donate their bodies or organs for research or transplantation. Consent may be given by a relative of a deceased person, but because relatives are often in shock or too upset to make such a decision, it is better to have one's intent made clear before death. This can be done by a statement in a will or by another signed document such as a Uniform Donor Card. The gift may be of all or part of one's body, and it may be made to a specific person such as a physician or an ill relative.

The document making the donation must be signed by the donor. If the donor is unable to sign, then the document must be signed by another individual before two witnesses, who must also sign in each other's presence and must state that they have done so.

The donor may designate in the document who the physician is that will carry out the procedure.

If the document or will has been delivered to a specific donee, it may be amended or revoked by the donor in the following ways:

- By executing a signed statement.
- By an oral statement made to two witnesses.

- By an oral statement during a terminal illness made to an attending physician.
- By executing and delivering a signed statement to the donee to whom the document of gift had previously been delivered.

If a document of gift has not been delivered to a donee, it may be revoked by any of the above methods or by destruction, cancellation, or mutilation of the document. It may also be revoked in the same method a will is revoked as described in chapter 5.

A Uniform Donor Card is included in appendix C as Form 19.

Appendix A
Glossary

administrator (administratrix if female). A person appointed by the court to oversee distribution of the property of someone who died (either without a will, or if the person designated in the will is unable to serve). However, in California today, this person is called a *personal representative*.

attested will. A will that includes an attestation clause and has been signed in front of witnesses.

beneficiary. A person who is entitled to receive property from a person who died (regardless of whether there is a will).

bequest. Personal property left to someone in a will.

children's trust. A trust set up to hold property given to children. Usually it provides that the children will not receive their property until they reach a higher age than the age of majority.

codicil. A change or amendment to a will.

community property. Property acquired by a husband and wife by their labors during their marriage.

decedent. A person who has died.

descendent. A child, grandchild, great-grandchild, etc.

devise. Real property left to someone in a will. A person who is entitled to a devise is called a *devisee*.

elective share. In non-community property states, the portion of the estate that may be taken by a surviving spouse, regardless of what the will states.

executor (**executrix** if female). A person appointed in a will to oversee distribution of the property of someone who died with a will. This person is also referred to as a *personal representative*.

exempt property. Property that is exempt from distribution as a normal part of the estate.

family allowance. An amount of money set aside from the estate to support the family of the decedent for a period of time.

forced share. See *elective share*.

heir. A person who will inherit from a decedent who died without a will.

holographic will. A will in which all of the material provisions are entirely in the handwriting of the maker. Holographic wills are valid in about half of the States including California.

intestate. Without making a will. One who dies without a will is said to have *died intestate*.

intestate share. In non-community property states, the portion of the estate a spouse is entitled to receive if there is no will.

joint tenancy. A type of property ownership by two or more persons, in which if one owner dies, that owner's interest automatically passes to the other joint tenants (not to the deceased owner's heirs as in tenancy in common).

legacy. Real property left to someone in a will. A person who is entitled to a legacy is called a *legatee*.

living will. A document expressing the writer's desires regarding how medical care is to be handled in the event the writer is not able to express his or her wishes concerning the use of life-prolonging medical procedures.

per capita. Distribution of property with equal shares going to each person.

per stirpes. Distribution of property with equal shares going to each family line.

personal representative. A person appointed by the court, or will, to oversee distribution of the property of the person who died. This is a more modern term than "administrator," "executor," etc., and applies regardless of whether there is a will.

probate. The process of settling a decedent's estate through the probate court.

residue. The property that is left over in an estate after all specific bequests and devises.

self-proving affidavit. A form added to a will in most states (but not required in California) in which the will maker and witnesses state under oath that they have signed and witnessed the will.

specific bequest or **specific devise**. A gift in a will of a specific item of property, or a specific amount of cash.

statutory will. A will which has been prepared according to the requirements of a statute.

tenancy by the entirety. A type of property ownership by a married couple, in which the property automatically passes to one spouse upon the death of the other. This is basically the same as joint tenancy, except that it is only between a husband and wife.

tenancy in common. Ownership of property by two or more people, in which each owner's share would descend to that owner's heirs (not to the other owners as in joint tenancy).

testate. With a will. One who dies with a will is said to have *died testate*.

testator. (**testatrix** if female.) A person who makes his or her will.

Appendix B
Sample Filled-in Forms

The following pages include sample filled-in forms for some of the wills in appendix C. They are filled out in different ways for different situations. You should look at all of them to see how the different sections can be completed.

FORM 6: SIMPLE WILL—Property to spouse **and** others. *This will should be used by persons who want their property to go to both their spouse and to other parties.*

FORM 11: SIMPLE WILL—(No spouse)—Property to minor children—two guardians. *This will is for persons who do not have a spouse and want all of their property to go to their children, at least one of whom is a minor. It provides for two guardians, one over the children and one over their estates.*

Form 15: SIMPLE WILL—No spouse and no children (to survivor). *Use this will if you have no spouse or children and want your property to go to the* survivor *of the people you name.*

FORM 17: CODICIL TO WILL. *This form can be used to change one section of a will. Usually it is just as easy to execute a new will, since all of the same formalities are required.*

FORM 18: LIVING WILL. *This form is used to state that you do not want your life artificially prolonged if you have a terminal illness or injury.*

Last Will and Testament

I, Chuck Didley a resident of San Mateo County, California do hereby make, publish, and declare this to be my Last Will and Testament, hereby revoking any and all Wills and Codicils heretofore made by me.

FIRST: I direct that all my just debts and funeral expenses be paid out of my estate as soon after my death as is practicable.

SECOND: I give, devise, and bequeath the following specific gifts:

Doe Didley, all Didley family photos.

Florida Sparks, my Harley Davidson motorcycle.

Donald Danker, my bowling trophies.

THIRD: I give, devise, and bequeath all my estate, real, personal, and mixed, of whatever kind and wherever situated, of which I may die seized or possessed, or in which I may have any interest or over which I may have any power of appointment or testamentary disposition, to my spouse, Ann Didley. If my said spouse does not survive me, I give, and bequeath the said property to Doe Didley and Florida Sparks in equal shares, or the survivor of them.

FOURTH: In the event that any beneficiary fails to survive me by thirty days, then this will shall take effect as if that person had predeceased me.

FIFTH: I hereby nominate, constitute, and appoint Julie Didley as Personal Representative of this, my Last Will and Testament. In the event that such named person is unable or unwilling to serve at any time or for any reason, then I nominate, constitute, and appoint Doe Didley as Personal Representative in the place and stead of the person first named herein. It is my will and I direct that my Personal Representative shall not be required to furnish a bond for the faithful performance of his or her duties in any jurisdiction, any provision of law to the contrary notwithstanding, and I give my Personal Representative full power to administer my estate, including the power to settle claims, pay debts, and sell, lease or exchange real and personal property without court order.

IN WITNESS WHEREOF I declare this to be my Last Will and Testament and execute it willingly as my free and voluntary act for the purposes expressed herein and I am of legal age and sound mind and make this under no constraint or undue influence, this 3rd day of August, 1999.

Chuck Didley L.S.

Each of us declares under penalty of perjury under the laws of the State of California that the following is true and correct:

The foregoing instrument was on said date subscribed at the end thereof by Chuck Didley, the above named Testator who signed, acknowledged, and published in the presence of us and each of us, who thereupon at his/her request, in his/her presence, and in the presence of each other, have hereunto subscribed our names as witnesses thereto. We are of sound mind and proper age to witness a will and understand this to be his/her will, and to the best of our knowledge testator is of legal age to make a will, of sound mind, and under no constraint or undue influence.

Jane K. Roe residing at Belmont, California

John V. Doe residing at San Carlos, California

Last Will and Testament

I, Sidney Falk a resident of Santa Clara County, California do hereby make, publish, and declare this to be my Last Will and Testament, hereby revoking any and all Wills and Codicils heretofore made by me.

FIRST: I direct that all my just debts and funeral expenses be paid out of my estate as soon after my death as is practicable.

SECOND: I give, devise, and bequeath the following specific gifts:
None --

THIRD: I give, devise, and bequeath all my estate, real, personal, and mixed, of whatever kind and wherever situated, of which I may die seized or possessed, or in which I may have any interest or over which I may have any power of appointment or testamentary disposition, to my children Jeffrey Falk, Brett Falk and Alan Falk --------, plus any afterborn or adopted children in equal shares or to their lineal descendants per stirpes.

FOURTH: In the event that any beneficiary fails to survive me by thirty days, then this will shall take effect as if that person had predeceased me.

FIFTH: In the event any of my children have not attained the age of 18 years at the time of my death, I hereby nominate, constitute, and appoint Brenda Fischer as guardian over the person of any of my children who have not reached the age of majority at the time of my death. In the event that said guardian is unable or unwilling to serve, then I nominate, constitute, and appoint Tom Fischer as guardian. Said guardian shall serve without bond or surety.

SIXTH: In the event any of my children have not attained the age of 18 years at the time of my death, I hereby nominate, constitute, and appoint Linda Stokes as guardian over the property of any of my children who have not reached the age of majority at the time of my death. In the event that said guardian is unable or unwilling to serve, then I nominate, constitute, and appoint Mark Stokes as guardian. Said guardian shall serve without bond or surety.

SEVENTH: I hereby nominate, constitute, and appoint Samuel Falk as Personal Representative of this, my Last Will and Testament. In the event that such named person is unable or unwilling to serve at any time or for any reason, then I nominate, constitute, and appoint Doug Schwinn as Personal Representative in the place and stead of the person first named herein. It is my will and I direct that my Personal Representative shall not be required to furnish a bond for the faithful performance of his or her duties in any jurisdiction, any provision of law to the contrary notwithstanding, and I give my Personal Representative full power to administer my estate, including the power to settle claims, pay debts, and sell, lease or exchange real and personal property without court order.

IN WITNESS WHEREOF I declare this to be my Last Will and Testament and execute it willingly as my free and voluntary act for the purposes expressed herein and I am of legal age and sound mind and make this under no constraint or undue influence, this 23rd day of May, 2001.

Sidney Falk L.S.

Each of us declares under penalty of perjury under the laws of the State of California that the following is true and correct:

The foregoing instrument was on said date subscribed at the end thereof by Sidney Falk, the above named Testator who signed, acknowledged, and published in the presence of us and each of us, who thereupon at his/her request, in his/her presence, and in the presence of each other, have hereunto subscribed our names as witnesses thereto. We are of sound mind and proper age to witness a will and understand this to be his/her will, and to the best of our knowledge testator is of legal age to make a will, of sound mind, and under no constraint or undue influence.

George C. Smith residing at Sunnyvale, California

Martha M. White residing at San Jose, California

Last Will and Testament

I, Kent Jones a resident of Marin County, California do hereby make, publish, and declare this to be my Last Will and Testament, hereby revoking any and all Wills and Codicils heretofore made by me.

FIRST: I direct that all my just debts and funeral expenses be paid out of my estate as soon after my death as is practicable.

SECOND: I give, devise, and bequeath the following specific gifts:
Joy Turner, all of my personal property located in my apartment.

THIRD: I give, devise, and bequeath all my estate, real, personal, and mixed, of whatever kind and wherever situated, of which I may die seized or possessed, or in which I may have any interest or over which I may have any power of appointment or testamentary disposition, to the following: The American Heart Association, Los Angeles Chapter

~~or to the survivor of them~~.

FOURTH: In the event that any beneficiary fails to survive me by thirty days, then this will shall take effect as if that person had predeceased me.

FIFTH: I hereby nominate, constitute, and appoint Joy Turner as Personal Representative of this, my Last Will and Testament. In the event that such named person is unable or unwilling to serve at any time or for any reason, then I nominate, constitute, and appoint Marianne Apple as Personal Representative in the place and stead of the person first named herein. It is my will and I direct that my Personal Representative shall not be required to furnish a bond for the faithful performance of his or her duties in any jurisdiction, any provision of law to the contrary notwithstanding, and I give my Personal Representative full power to administer my estate, including the power to settle claims, pay debts, and sell, lease or exchange real and personal property without court order.

IN WITNESS WHEREOF I declare this to be my Last Will and Testament and execute it willingly as my free and voluntary act for the purposes expressed herein and I am of legal age and sound mind and make this under no constraint or undue influence, this 3rd day of June, 2000.

Kent Jones L.S.

Each of us declares under penalty of perjury under the laws of the State of California that the following is true and correct:

The foregoing instrument was on said date subscribed at the end thereof by ________Kent Jones________, the above named Testator who signed, acknowledged, and published in the presence of us and each of us, who thereupon at his/her request, in his/her presence, and in the presence of each other, have hereunto subscribed our names as witnesses thereto. We are of sound mind and proper age to witness a will and understand this to be his/her will, and to the best of our knowledge testator is of legal age to make a will, of sound mind, and under no constraint or undue influence.

Melissa A. Brown residing at Marin, California

Joyce P. Carlyle residing at San Rafael, California

Codicil to the Will of

Kent Jones

I, Kent Jones, a resident of Marin County, California declare this to be the first codicil to my Last Will and Testament dated June 3, 2000.

FIRST: I hereby revoke the clause of my Will which reads as follows: SECOND: I give, devise, and bequeath the following specific gifts: Joy Turner, all of my personal property located in my apartment.

SECOND: I hereby add the following clause to my Will: SECOND: I give, devise, and bequeath the following specific gifts: Joy Turner, 50% of my personal property located in my apartment, and Rob Roy, 50% of my personal property located in my apartment, or the survivor of them.

THIRD: In all other respects I hereby confirm and republish my Last Will and Testament dated June 3, 2000.

IN WITNESS WHEREOF, I have signed, published, and declared the foregoing instrument as and for a codicil to my Last Will and Testament, this 6th day of August, 2002.

Kent Jones

The foregoing instrument was on the 6 day of August, 2002, signed at the end thereof, and at the same time published and declared by Kent Jones, as and for a codicil to his/her Last Will and Testament, dated June 3, 2000, in the presence of each of us, who, this attestation clause having been read to us, did at the request of the said testator/testatrix, in his/her presence and in the presence of each other signed our names as witnesses thereto.

Heather E. Anderson residing at Marin, California

John H. Atman residing at Sausalito, California

Living Will

Declaration made this 3rd day of June, 1999.

I, Cindy Cane, willfully and voluntarily make known that my life not be artificially prolonged under the circumstances set forth below.

If at any time I have a terminal condition and if my attending or treating physician and another consulting physician have determined that there can be no medical probability of my recovery from such condition, I direct my attending physician, pursuant to the Natural Death Act of California, to withhold or withdraw life-prolonging procedures when the application of such procedures would serve only to prolong artificially the process of dying, and that I be permitted to die naturally.

In the absence of my ability to give directions on the use of such life-prolonging procedures, it is my intention that this declaration be honored by my family and physician as the final expression of my legal right to refuse medical or surgical treatment and to accept the consequences for such refusal.

If I have been diagnosed as pregnant, and that diagnosis is known to my physician, this declaration shall have no force or effect during my pregnancy.

I understand the full import of this declaration, and am emotionally and mentally competent to make this declaration.

Additional Instructions (optional):

____

____

____

Cindy Cane

Signature

555 Palm Street,

Address

San Mateo, CA 94403

The declarant voluntarily signed this writing in my presence. I am not entitled to any portion of the declarant's estate upon his or her death. I am not a health care provider, the operator of a community care facility, the operator of a residential care facility for the elderly or an employee of any of the above.

Mary L. Pollare

Witness

123 Jerry Place,

San Mateo, CA 94404

Address

The declarant voluntarily signed this writing in my presence. I am not entitled to any portion of the declarant's estate upon his or her death. I am not a health care provider, the operator of a community care facility, the operator of a residential care facility for the elderly or an employee of any of the above.

Karen J. Previn

Witness

4400 Northridge Circle,

San Mateo, CA 94400

Address

Appendix C
Forms

The following pages contain forms that can be used to prepare a will, codicil, living will, and Uniform Donor Card. They should only be used by persons who have read this book, who do not have any complications in their legal affairs, and who understand the forms they are using. The forms may be used right out of the book or they may be photocopied or retyped.

Form 1. Asset and Beneficiary List—*Use this form to keep an accurate record of your estate as well as your beneficiaries' names and addresses.*

Form 2. Preferences and Information List—*Use this form to let your family know of your wishes on matters not usually included in a will.*

Form 3. Simple Will—Spouse and Minor Children—One Guardian. *Use this will if you have minor children and want all your property to go to your spouse, but if your spouse dies previously, then to your minor children. It provides for one person to be guardian over your children and their estates.*

Form 4. Simple Will—Spouse and Minor Children—Two Guardians. *Use this will if you have minor children and want all your property to go to your spouse, but if your spouse dies previously, then to your minor children. It provides for two guardians, one over your children and one over their estates.*

Form 5. Simple Will—Spouse and Minor Children—Guardian and Trust. *This will should be used if you have minor children and want all your property to go to your spouse, but if your spouse dies previously, then to your minor children. It provides for one person to be guardian over your children and for either the same person or another to be trustee over their property. This will allows your children's property to be held until they are older than eighteen rather than distributing it all to them at age eighteen.*

Form 6. Simple Will—Spouse and no children. *Use this will if you want your property to go to your spouse but if your spouse predeceases you, to others or the* survivor *of the others.*

Form 7. Simple Will—Spouse and no children. *Use this will if you want your property to go to your spouse but if your spouse predeceases you, to others or the* descendants *of the others.*

Form 8. Simple Will—Spouse and Adult Children. *Use this will if you want all of your property to go to your spouse, but if your spouse dies previously, then to your children, all of whom are adults.*

Form 9. Simple Will—Spouse and Adult Children. *Use this will if you want some of your property to go to your spouse, and some of your property to your children, all of whom are adults.*

Form 10. Simple Will—No Spouse—Minor Children—One Guardian. *Use this will if you do not have a spouse and want all your property to go to your children, at least one of whom is a minor. It provides for one person to be guardian over your children and their estates.*

Form 11. Simple Will—No Spouse—Minor Children—Two Guardians. *Use this will if you do not have a spouse and want all your property to go to your children, at least one of whom is a minor. It provides for two guardians, one over your children and one over their estates.*

Form 12. Simple Will—No Spouse—Minor Children—Guardian and Trust. *Use this will if you do not have a spouse and want all your property to go to your children, at least one of whom is a minor. It provides for one person to be guardian over your children and for either that person or another to be trustee over their property. This will allows your children's property to be held until they are older than eighteen rather than distributing it all to them at age eighteen.*

Form 13. Simple Will—No Spouse—Adult Children. *This will should be used if you wish to leave your property to your adult children, or equally to each* family *if they predecease you.*

Form 14. Simple Will—No Spouse—Adult Children. *This will should be used if you wish to leave your property to your adult children, or equally to each* person *if they predecease you.*

Form 15. Simple Will—No spouse and no children. *Use this will if you have no spouse or children and want your property to go to the* survivor *of the people you name.*

Form 16. Simple Will—No spouse and no children. *Use this will if you have no spouse or children and want your property to go to the* descendants *of the people you name.*

Form 17. Codicil to Will. *This form can be used to change one section of your will. Usually it is just as easy to execute a new will, since all of the same formalities are required.*

Form 18. Living Will. *This is a document which expresses your desire to withhold certain extraordinary medical treatment should you have a terminal illness and you reach such a state that your wishes to withhold such treatment cannot be determined.*

Form 19. Organ Donor Card. *This form is used to spell out your wishes for donation of your body or any organs.*

How to Pick the Right Will

Follow the chart and use the form number in the black circle.

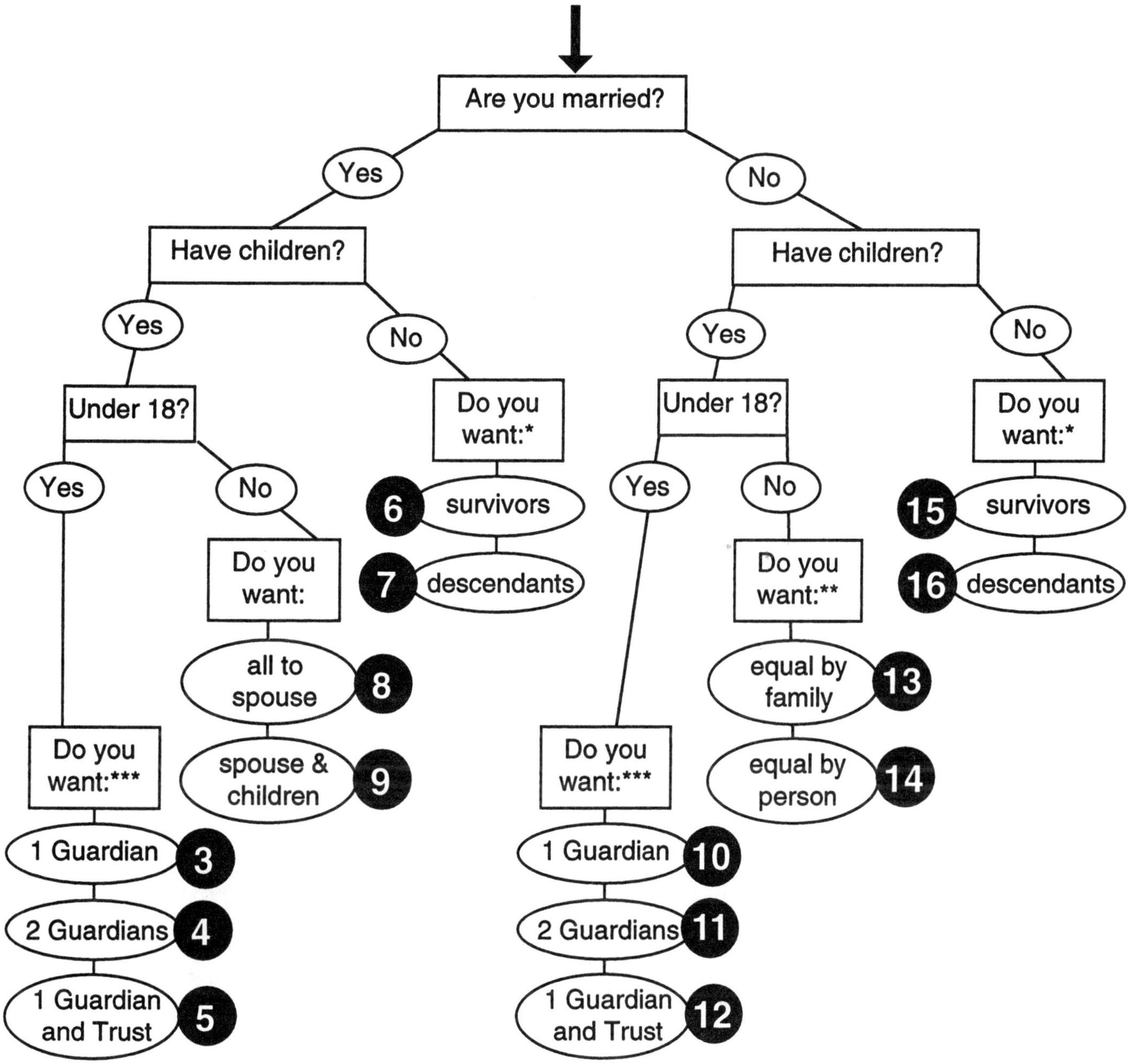

* For an explanation of survivors/decendants see page 25

** For an explanation of families/persons see page 25

*** For an explanation of childrens' guardians and trust, see pages 27 and 28

Asset and Beneficiary List

Property Inventory

Assets

Bank Accounts (checking, savings, certificates of deposit)

Real Estate

Vehicles (cars, trucks, boats, planes, RVs, etc.)

Personal Property (collections, jewelry, tools, artwork, household items, etc.)

Stocks/Bonds/Mutual Funds

Retirement Accounts (IRAs, 401(k)s, pension plans, etc.)

Receivables (mortgages held, notes, accounts receivable, personal loans)

Life Insurance

Other Property (trusts, partnerships, businesses, profit sharing, copyrights, etc.)

Liabilities

Real Estate Loans

Vehicle Loans

Other Secured Loans

Unsecured Loans and Debts (taxes, child support, judgments, etc.)

Beneficiary List

Name____________________ Address____________________ Phone__________

Preferences and Information List

Statement of Desires and Location of Property & Documents

I, ______________________________, am signing this document as the expression of my desires as to the matters stated below, and to inform my family members or other significant persons of the location of certain property and documents in the event of any emergency or of my death.

1. **Funeral Desires.** It is my desire that the following arrangements be made for my funeral and disposition of remains in the event of my death (state if you have made any arrangements, such as pre-paid burial plans, cemetery plots owned, etc.):

- ❏ Burial at ______________________________
  ______________________________.
- ❏ Cremation at ______________________________
  ______________________________.
- ❏ Other specific desires: ______________________________
  ____
  ______________________________.

2. **Pets.** I have the following pet(s): ______________________________
______________________________. The following are my desires concerning the care of said pet(s): ______________________________
____
______________________________.

3. **Notification.** I would like the following person(s) notified in the event of emergency or death (give name, address and phone number):

____
____
____
____
______________________________.

4. **Location of Documents.** The following is a list of important documents, and their location:

- ❏ Last Will and Testament, dated ______________. Location: ____________
  ______________________________.
- ❏ Durable Power of Attorney, dated ______________. Location: ____________
  ______________________________.
- ❏ Living Will, dated ______________. Location: ______________
  ______________________________.
- ❏ Deed(s) to real estate (describe property location and location of deed):
  ____
  ____
  ____

❏ Title(s) to vehicles (cars, boats, etc.) (Describe vehicle, its location, and location of title, registration, or other documents):

____
____
____
____

❏ Life insurance policies (list name address & phone number of insurance company and insurance agent, policy number, and location of policy):

____
____
____

❏ Other insurance policies (list type, company & agent, policy number, and location of policy):

____
____
____

❏ Other: (list other documents such as stock certificates, bonds, certificates of deposit, etc., and their location):

____
____
____

5. **Location of Assets.** In addition to items readily visible in my home or listed above, I have the following assets:

❏ Safe deposit box located at __________, box number _____. Key located at: _____.

❏ Bank accounts (list name & address of bank, type of account, and account number):

____

❏ Other (describe the item and give its location):

____
____
____
____
____

6. Other desires or information (state any desires or provide any information not given above; use additional sheets of paper if necessary):

____
____
____
____
____

Dated: ________________________

____
Signature

Last Will and Testament

I, ______________________________ a resident of ____________________ County, California do hereby make, publish, and declare this to be my Last Will and Testament, hereby revoking any and all Wills and Codicils heretofore made by me.

FIRST: I direct that all my just debts and funeral expenses be paid out of my estate as soon after my death as is practicable.

SECOND: I give, devise, and bequeath the following specific gifts:

____

____

____

____

____

____

____

____

____

____

THIRD: I give, devise, and bequeath all my estate, real, personal, and mixed, of whatever kind and wherever situated, of which I may die seized or possessed, or in which I may have any interest or over which I may have any power of appointment or testamentary disposition, to my spouse, ______________________________. If my said spouse does not survive me, I give, and bequeath the said property to my children ______________________________

____

____,

plus any afterborn or adopted children in equal shares or their lineal descendants, per stirpes.

FOURTH: In the event that any beneficiary fails to survive me by thirty days, then this will shall take effect as if that person had predeceased me.

FIFTH: Should my spouse not survive me, I hereby nominate, constitute, and appoint ______________________________ as guardian over the person and estate of any of my children who have not reached the age of majority at the time of my death. In the event that said guardian is unable or unwilling to serve, then I nominate, constitute, and appoint ______________________________ as guardian. Said guardian shall serve without bond or surety.

SIXTH: I hereby nominate, constitute, and appoint ______________________________ as Personal Representative of this, my Last Will and Testament. In the event that such named person is unable or unwilling to serve at any time or for any reason, then I nominate, constitute, and appoint ______________________________ as Personal Representative in the place and stead of the person first named herein. It is my will and I direct that my Personal Representative shall not be required to furnish a bond for the faithful performance of his or her duties in any jurisdiction, any provision of law to the contrary notwithstanding, and I give my Personal Representative full power to administer my estate, including the power to settle claims, pay debts, and sell, lease or exchange real and personal property without court order.

IN WITNESS WHEREOF I declare this to be my Last Will and Testament and execute it willingly as my free and voluntary act for the purposes expressed herein and I am of legal age and sound mind and make this under no constraint or undue influence, this _____ day of __________________, ______.

____L.S.

Each of us declares under penalty of perjury under the laws of the State of California that the following is true and correct:

The foregoing instrument was on said date subscribed at the end thereof by ____, the above named Testator who signed, acknowledged, and published in the presence of us and each of us, who thereupon at his/her request, in his/her presence, and in the presence of each other, have hereunto subscribed our names as witnesses thereto. We are of sound mind and proper age to witness a will and understand this to be his/her will, and to the best of our knowledge testator is of legal age to make a will, of sound mind, and under no constraint or undue influence.

____residing at____

____residing at____

Last Will and Testament

I, ______________________________ a resident of ____________________ County, California do hereby make, publish, and declare this to be my Last Will and Testament, hereby revoking any and all Wills and Codicils heretofore made by me.

FIRST: I direct that all my just debts and funeral expenses be paid out of my estate as soon after my death as is practicable.

SECOND: I give, devise, and bequeath the following specific gifts:

____

____

____

____

____

____

____

____

____

____

THIRD: I give, devise, and bequeath all my estate, real, personal, and mixed, of whatever kind and wherever situated, of which I may die seized or possessed, or in which I may have any interest or over which I may have any power of appointment or testamentary disposition, to my spouse, ______________________________. If my said spouse does not survive me, I give, and bequeath the said property to my children ______________________________

____

____,

plus any afterborn or adopted children in equal shares or their lineal descendants, per stirpes.

FOURTH: In the event that any beneficiary fails to survive me by thirty days, then this will shall take effect as if that person had predeceased me.

FIFTH: Should my spouse not survive me, I hereby nominate, constitute, and appoint ______________________________, as guardian over the person of any of my children who have not reached the age of majority at the time of my death. In the event that said guardian is unable or unwilling to serve, then I nominate, constitute, and appoint ______________________________ as guardian. Said guardian shall serve without bond or surety.

SIXTH: Should my spouse not survive me, I hereby nominate, constitute, and appoint ______________________________ as guardian over the estate of any of my children who have not reached the age of majority at the time of my death. In the event that said guardian is unable or unwilling to serve, then I nominate, constitute, and appoint ______________________________ as guardian. Said guardian shall serve without bond or surety.

SEVENTH: I hereby nominate, constitute, and appoint ______________________________ as Personal Representative of this, my Last Will and Testament. In the event that such named person is unable or unwilling to serve at any time or for any reason, then I nominate, constitute, and appoint ______________________________ as Personal Representative in the place and stead of the person first named herein. It is my will and I direct that my Personal Representative shall not be required to furnish a bond for the faithful performance of his or her duties in any jurisdiction, any provision of law to the contrary notwithstanding, and I give my Personal Representative full power to administer my estate, including the power to settle claims, pay debts, and sell, lease or exchange real and personal property without court order.

IN WITNESS WHEREOF I declare this to be my Last Will and Testament and execute it willingly as my free and voluntary act for the purposes expressed herein and I am of legal age and sound mind and make this under no constraint or undue influence, this _____ day of ________________, ______.

______________________________L.S.

Each of us declares under penalty of perjury under the laws of the State of California that the following is true and correct:

The foregoing instrument was on said date subscribed at the end thereof by ______________________________, the above named Testator who signed, acknowledged, and published in the presence of us and each of us, who thereupon at his/her request, in his/her presence, and in the presence of each other, have hereunto subscribed our names as witnesses thereto. We are of sound mind and proper age to witness a will and understand this to be his/her will, and to the best of our knowledge testator is of legal age to make a will, of sound mind, and under no constraint or undue influence.

______________________________residing at______________________________

______________________________residing at______________________________

Last Will and Testament

I, ______________________________________ a resident of ______________________ County, California do hereby make, publish, and declare this to be my Last Will and Testament, hereby revoking any and all Wills and Codicils heretofore made by me.

FIRST: I direct that all my just debts and funeral expenses be paid out of my estate as soon after my death as is practicable.

SECOND: I give, devise, and bequeath the following specific gifts:

____

____

____

____

____

____

____

____

____

____

THIRD: I give, devise, and bequeath all my estate, real, personal, and mixed, of whatever kind and wherever situated, of which I may die seized or possessed, or in which I may have any interest or over which I may have any power of appointment or testamentary disposition, to my spouse, ____. If my said spouse does not survive me, I give, and bequeath the said property to my children ______________________________________

____

____,

plus any afterborn or adopted children in equal shares or their lineal descendants, per stirpes.

FOURTH: In the event that any beneficiary fails to survive me by thirty days, then this will shall take effect as if that person had predeceased me.

FIFTH: In the event that any of my children have not reached the age of ________ years at the time of my death, then the share of any such child shall be held in a separate trust by ____________________________________ for such child.

The trustee shall use the income and that part of the principal of the trust as is, in the trustee's sole discretion, necessary or desirable to provide proper housing, medical care, food, clothing, entertainment and education for the trust beneficiary, considering the beneficiary's other resources. Any income that is not distributed shall be added to the principal. Additionally, the trustee shall have all powers conferred by the law of the state having jurisdiction over this trust, as well as the power to pay from the assets of the trust reasonable fees necessary to administer the trust.

The trust shall terminate when the child reaches the age specified above and the remaining assets distributed to the child, unless they have been exhausted sooner. In the event the child dies prior to the termination of the trust, then the assets shall pass to the estate of the child. The interests of the beneficiary under this trust shall not be assignable and shall be free from the claims of creditors to the full extent allowed by law.

In the event the said trustee is unable or unwilling to serve for any reason, then I nominate, constitute, and appoint ____ as alternate trustee. No bond shall be required of either trustee in any jurisdiction and this trust shall be administered without court supervision as allowed by law.

SIXTH: Should my spouse not survive me, I hereby nominate, constitute, and appoint ____________________________________ as guardian over the person and estate of any of my children who have not reached the age of majority at the time of my death. In the event that said guardian is unable or unwilling to serve, then I nominate, constitute, and appoint ____ as guardian.

SEVENTH: I hereby nominate, constitute, and appoint ____________________________ as Personal Representative of this, my Last Will and Testament. In the event that such named person is unable or unwilling to serve at any time or for any reason, then I nominate, constitute, and appoint ______________________________ as Personal Representative in the place and stead of the person first named herein. It is my will and I direct that my Personal Representative shall not be required to furnish a bond for the faithful performance of his or her duties in any jurisdiction, any provision of law to the contrary notwithstanding, and I give my Personal Representative full power to administer my estate, including the power to settle claims, pay debts, and sell, lease or exchange real and personal property without court order.

IN WITNESS WHEREOF I declare this to be my Last Will and Testament and execute it willingly as my free and voluntary act for the purposes expressed herein and I am of legal age and sound mind and make this under no constraint or undue influence, this _____ day of __________________, ______.

__________________________________ L.S.

Each of us declares under penalty of perjury under the laws of the State of California that the following is true and correct:

The foregoing instrument was on said date subscribed at the end thereof by ____________________________________, the above named Testator who signed, acknowledged, and published in the presence of us and each of us, who thereupon at his/her request, in his/her presence, and in the presence of each other, have hereunto subscribed our names as witnesses thereto. We are of sound mind and proper age to witness a will and understand this to be his/her will, and to the best of our knowledge testator is of legal age to make a will, of sound mind, and under no constraint or undue influence.

____________________________________ residing at ____________________________________

____________________________________ residing at ____________________________________

Last Will and Testament

I, ______________________________________ a resident of ____________________ County, California do hereby make, publish, and declare this to be my Last Will and Testament, hereby revoking any and all Wills and Codicils heretofore made by me.

FIRST: I direct that all my just debts and funeral expenses be paid out of my estate as soon after my death as is practicable.

SECOND: I give, devise, and bequeath the following specific gifts:

____

____

____

____

____

____

____

____

____

____

THIRD: I give, devise, and bequeath all my estate, real, personal, and mixed, of whatever kind and wherever situated, of which I may die seized or possessed, or in which I may have any interest or over which I may have any power of appointment or testamentary disposition, to my spouse, ____. If my said spouse does not survive me, I give, and bequeath the said property to ____

____

____, or the survivor of them.

FOURTH: In the event that any beneficiary fails to survive me by thirty days, then this will shall take effect as if that person had predeceased me.

FIFTH: I hereby nominate, constitute, and appoint ______________________________ as Personal Representative of this, my Last Will and Testament. In the event that such named person is unable or unwilling to serve at any time or for any reason, then I nominate, constitute, and appoint ________________________________ as Personal Representative in the place and stead of the person first named herein. It is my will and I direct that my Personal Representative shall not be required to furnish a bond for the faithful performance of his or her duties in any jurisdiction, any provision of law to the contrary notwithstanding, and I give my Personal Representative full power to administer my estate, including the power to settle claims, pay debts, and sell, lease or exchange real and personal property without court order.

IN WITNESS WHEREOF I declare this to be my Last Will and Testament and execute it willingly as my free and voluntary act for the purposes expressed herein and I am of legal age and

sound mind and make this under no constraint or undue influence, this _____ day of ________________, ______.

___________________________________L.S.

Each of us declares under penalty of perjury under the laws of the State of California that the following is true and correct:

The foregoing instrument was on said date subscribed at the end thereof by ____________________________________, the above named Testator who signed, acknowledged, and published in the presence of us and each of us, who thereupon at his/her request, in his/her presence, and in the presence of each other, have hereunto subscribed our names as witnesses thereto. We are of sound mind and proper age to witness a will and understand this to be his/her will, and to the best of our knowledge testator is of legal age to make a will, of sound mind, and under no constraint or undue influence.

____________________________________residing at_________________________________

____________________________________residing at_________________________________

Last Will and Testament

I, ______________________________________ a resident of ____________________ County, California do hereby make, publish, and declare this to be my Last Will and Testament, hereby revoking any and all Wills and Codicils heretofore made by me.

FIRST: I direct that all my just debts and funeral expenses be paid out of my estate as soon after my death as is practicable.

SECOND: I give, devise, and bequeath the following specific gifts:

____

____

____

____

____

____

____

____

____

____

THIRD: I give, devise, and bequeath all my estate, real, personal, and mixed, of whatever kind and wherever situated, of which I may die seized or possessed, or in which I may have any interest or over which I may have any power of appointment or testamentary disposition, to my spouse, ____. If my said spouse does not survive me, I give, and bequeath the said property to ____

____

____,

or to their lineal descendants, per stirpes.

FOURTH: In the event that any beneficiary fails to survive me by thirty days, then this will shall take effect as if that person had predeceased me.

FIFTH: I hereby nominate, constitute, and appoint ______________________________ as Personal Representative of this, my Last Will and Testament. In the event that such named person is unable or unwilling to serve at any time or for any reason, then I nominate, constitute, and appoint ______________________________ as Personal Representative in the place and stead of the person first named herein. It is my will and I direct that my Personal Representative shall not be required to furnish a bond for the faithful performance of his or her duties in any jurisdiction, any provision of law to the contrary notwithstanding, and I give my Personal Representative full power to administer my estate, including the power to settle claims, pay debts, and sell, lease or exchange real and personal property without court order.

IN WITNESS WHEREOF I declare this to be my Last Will and Testament and execute it willingly as my free and voluntary act for the purposes expressed herein and I am of legal age and

sound mind and make this under no constraint or undue influence, this _____ day of _________________, ______.

__________________________________L.S.

Each of us declares under penalty of perjury under the laws of the State of California that the following is true and correct:

The foregoing instrument was on said date subscribed at the end thereof by _______________________________________, the above named Testator who signed, acknowledged, and published in the presence of us and each of us, who thereupon at his/her request, in his/her presence, and in the presence of each other, have hereunto subscribed our names as witnesses thereto. We are of sound mind and proper age to witness a will and understand this to be his/her will, and to the best of our knowledge testator is of legal age to make a will, of sound mind, and under no constraint or undue influence.

_______________________________________residing at_____________________________________

_______________________________________residing at_____________________________________

Last Will and Testament

I, ______________________________________ a resident of ______________________ County, California do hereby make, publish, and declare this to be my Last Will and Testament, hereby revoking any and all Wills and Codicils heretofore made by me.

FIRST: I direct that all my just debts and funeral expenses be paid out of my estate as soon after my death as is practicable.

SECOND: I give, devise, and bequeath the following specific gifts:

____

____

____

____

____

____

____

____

____

____

THIRD: I give, devise, and bequeath all my estate, real, personal, and mixed, of whatever kind and wherever situated, of which I may die seized or possessed, or in which I may have any interest or over which I may have any power of appointment or testamentary disposition, to my spouse, ______________________________________. If my said spouse does not survive me, I give, and bequeath the said property to my children ____________________________________

____

____,

in equal shares or to their lineal descendants, per stirpes.

FOURTH: In the event that any beneficiary fails to survive me by thirty days, then this will shall take effect as if that person had predeceased me.

FIFTH: I hereby nominate, constitute, and appoint ______________________________ as Personal Representative of this, my Last Will and Testament. In the event that such named person is unable or unwilling to serve at any time or for any reason, then I nominate, constitute, and appoint ______________________________ as Personal Representative in the place and stead of the person first named herein. It is my will and I direct that my Personal Representative shall not be required to furnish a bond for the faithful performance of his or her duties in any jurisdiction, any provision of law to the contrary notwithstanding, and I give my Personal Representative full power to administer my estate, including the power to settle claims, pay debts, and sell, lease or exchange real and personal property without court order.

IN WITNESS WHEREOF I declare this to be my Last Will and Testament and execute it willingly as my free and voluntary act for the purposes expressed herein and I am of legal age and

sound mind and make this under no constraint or undue influence, this _____ day of __________________, ______.

____________________________________L.S.

Each of us declares under penalty of perjury under the laws of the State of California that the following is true and correct:

The foregoing instrument was on said date subscribed at the end thereof by ____, the above named Testator who signed, acknowledged, and published in the presence of us and each of us, who thereupon at his/her request, in his/her presence, and in the presence of each other, have hereunto subscribed our names as witnesses thereto. We are of sound mind and proper age to witness a will and understand this to be his/her will, and to the best of our knowledge testator is of legal age to make a will, of sound mind, and under no constraint or undue influence.

____residing at_____________________________________

____residing at_____________________________________

Last Will and Testament

I, ______________________________________ a resident of ______________________ County, California do hereby make, publish, and declare this to be my Last Will and Testament, hereby revoking any and all Wills and Codicils heretofore made by me.

FIRST: I direct that all my just debts and funeral expenses be paid out of my estate as soon after my death as is practicable.

SECOND: I give, devise, and bequeath the following specific gifts:

____

____

____

____

____

____

____

____

____

____

THIRD: I give, devise, and bequeath all my estate, real, personal, and mixed, of whatever kind and wherever situated, of which I may die seized or possessed, or in which I may have any interest or over which I may have any power of appointment or testamentary disposition, as follows:

_______% to my spouse, ____ and

_______% to my children, ____

____

____,

in equal shares or to their lineal descendants per stirpes.

FOURTH: In the event that any beneficiary fails to survive me by thirty days, then this will shall take effect as if that person had predeceased me.

FIFTH: I hereby nominate, constitute, and appoint ________________________________ as Personal Representative of this, my Last Will and Testament. In the event that such named person is unable or unwilling to serve at any time or for any reason, then I nominate, constitute, and appoint ________________________________ as Personal Representative in the place and stead of the person first named herein. It is my will and I direct that my Personal Representative shall not be required to furnish a bond for the faithful performance of his or her duties in any jurisdiction, any provision of law to the contrary notwithstanding, and I give my Personal Representative full power to administer my estate, including the power to settle claims, pay debts, and sell, lease or exchange real and personal property without court order.

IN WITNESS WHEREOF I declare this to be my Last Will and Testament and execute it willingly as my free and voluntary act for the purposes expressed herein and I am of legal age and

sound mind and make this under no constraint or undue influence, this _____ day of ________________, ______.

_____________________________________L.S.

Each of us declares under penalty of perjury under the laws of the State of California that the following is true and correct:

The foregoing instrument was on said date subscribed at the end thereof by ______________________________________, the above named Testator who signed, acknowledged, and published in the presence of us and each of us, who thereupon at his/her request, in his/her presence, and in the presence of each other, have hereunto subscribed our names as witnesses thereto. We are of sound mind and proper age to witness a will and understand this to be his/her will, and to the best of our knowledge testator is of legal age to make a will, of sound mind, and under no constraint or undue influence.

______________________________________residing at___________________________________

______________________________________residing at___________________________________

Last Will and Testament

I, ______________________________ a resident of ________________ County, California do hereby make, publish, and declare this to be my Last Will and Testament, hereby revoking any and all Wills and Codicils heretofore made by me.

FIRST: I direct that all my just debts and funeral expenses be paid out of my estate as soon after my death as is practicable.

SECOND: I give, devise, and bequeath the following specific gifts:

____

____

____

____

____

____

____

____

____

____

THIRD: I give, devise, and bequeath all my estate, real, personal, and mixed, of whatever kind and wherever situated, of which I may die seized or possessed, or in which I may have any interest or over which I may have any power of appointment or testamentary disposition, to my children ____

____

____, plus any afterborn or adopted children in equal shares or to their lineal descendants per stirpes.

FOURTH: In the event that any beneficiary fails to survive me by thirty days, then this will shall take effect as if that person had predeceased me.

FIFTH: In the event any of my children have not attained the age of 18 years at the time of my death, I hereby nominate, constitute, and appoint ______________________________ as guardian over the person and estate of any of my children who have not reached the age of majority at the time of my death. In the event that said guardian is unable or unwilling to serve, then I nominate, constitute, and appoint ______________________________ as guardian. Said guardian shall serve without bond or surety.

SIXTH: I hereby nominate, constitute, and appoint ______________________________ as Personal Representative of this, my Last Will and Testament. In the event that such named person is unable or unwilling to serve at any time or for any reason, then I nominate, constitute, and appoint ______________________________ as Personal Representative in the place and stead of the person first named herein. It is my will and I direct that my Personal Representative shall not be required to furnish a bond for the faithful performance of his or her duties in any jurisdiction, any

provision of law to the contrary notwithstanding, and I give my Personal Representative full power to administer my estate, including the power to settle claims, pay debts, and sell, lease or exchange real and personal property without court order.

IN WITNESS WHEREOF I declare this to be my Last Will and Testament and execute it willingly as my free and voluntary act for the purposes expressed herein and I am of legal age and sound mind and make this under no constraint or undue influence, this _____ day of __________________, ______.

____________________________________L.S.

Each of us declares under penalty of perjury under the laws of the State of California that the following is true and correct:

The foregoing instrument was on said date subscribed at the end thereof by ____, the above named Testator who signed, acknowledged, and published in the presence of us and each of us, who thereupon at his/her request, in his/her presence, and in the presence of each other, have hereunto subscribed our names as witnesses thereto. We are of sound mind and proper age to witness a will and understand this to be his/her will, and to the best of our knowledge testator is of legal age to make a will, of sound mind, and under no constraint or undue influence.

____residing at____________________________________

____residing at____________________________________

Last Will and Testament

I, ______________________________ a resident of ____________________ County, California do hereby make, publish, and declare this to be my Last Will and Testament, hereby revoking any and all Wills and Codicils heretofore made by me.

FIRST: I direct that all my just debts and funeral expenses be paid out of my estate as soon after my death as is practicable.

SECOND: I give, devise, and bequeath the following specific gifts:

____

____

____

____

____

____

____

____

____

____

THIRD: I give, devise, and bequeath all my estate, real, personal, and mixed, of whatever kind and wherever situated, of which I may die seized or possessed, or in which I may have any interest or over which I may have any power of appointment or testamentary disposition, to my children ____

____

____, plus any afterborn or adopted children in equal shares or to their lineal descendants per stirpes.

FOURTH: In the event that any beneficiary fails to survive me by thirty days, then this will shall take effect as if that person had predeceased me.

FIFTH: In the event any of my children have not attained the age of 18 years at the time of my death, I hereby nominate, constitute, and appoint ______________________________ as guardian over the person of any of my children who have not reached the age of majority at the time of my death. In the event that said guardian is unable or unwilling to serve, then I nominate, constitute, and appoint ______________________________ as guardian. Said guardian shall serve without bond or surety.

SIXTH: In the event any of my children have not attained the age of 18 years at the time of my death, I hereby nominate, constitute, and appoint ______________________________ as guardian over the property of any of my children who have not reached the age of majority at the time of my death. In the event that said guardian is unable or unwilling to serve, then I nominate, constitute, and appoint ______________________________ as guardian. Said guardian shall serve without bond or surety.

SEVENTH: I hereby nominate, constitute, and appoint ______________________ as Personal Representative of this, my Last Will and Testament. In the event that such named person is unable or unwilling to serve at any time or for any reason, then I nominate, constitute, and appoint ______________________________ as Personal Representative in the place and stead of the person first named herein. It is my will and I direct that my Personal Representative shall not be required to furnish a bond for the faithful performance of his or her duties in any jurisdiction, any provision of law to the contrary notwithstanding, and I give my Personal Representative full power to administer my estate, including the power to settle claims, pay debts, and sell, lease or exchange real and personal property without court order.

IN WITNESS WHEREOF I declare this to be my Last Will and Testament and execute it willingly as my free and voluntary act for the purposes expressed herein and I am of legal age and sound mind and make this under no constraint or undue influence, this _____ day of ________________, ______.

__________________________________L.S.

Each of us declares under penalty of perjury under the laws of the State of California that the following is true and correct:

The foregoing instrument was on said date subscribed at the end thereof by ____________________________________, the above named Testator who signed, acknowledged, and published in the presence of us and each of us, who thereupon at his/her request, in his/her presence, and in the presence of each other, have hereunto subscribed our names as witnesses thereto. We are of sound mind and proper age to witness a will and understand this to be his/her will, and to the best of our knowledge testator is of legal age to make a will, of sound mind, and under no constraint or undue influence.

____________________________________residing at__________________________________

____________________________________residing at__________________________________

Last Will and Testament

I, ______________________________ a resident of ____________________ County, California do hereby make, publish, and declare this to be my Last Will and Testament, hereby revoking any and all Wills and Codicils heretofore made by me.

FIRST: I direct that all my just debts and funeral expenses be paid out of my estate as soon after my death as is practicable.

SECOND: I give, devise, and bequeath the following specific gifts:
____
____
____
____
____
____
____
____
____
____

THIRD: I give, devise, and bequeath all my estate, real, personal, and mixed, of whatever kind and wherever situated, of which I may die seized or possessed, or in which I may have any interest or over which I may have any power of appointment or testamentary disposition, to my children ____
____
____,
plus any afterborn or adopted children in equal shares or to their lineal descendants per stirpes.

FOURTH: In the event that any beneficiary fails to survive me by thirty days, then this will shall take effect as if that person had predeceased me.

FIFTH: In the event that any of my children have not reached the age of ________ years at the time of my death, then the share of any such child shall be held in a separate trust by ______________________________ for such child.

The trustee shall use the income and that part of the principal of the trust as is, in the trustee's sole discretion, necessary or desirable to provide proper housing, medical care, food, clothing, entertainment and education for the trust beneficiary, considering the beneficiary's other resources. Any income that is not distributed shall be added to the principal. Additionally, the trustee shall have all powers conferred by the law of the state having jurisdiction over this trust, as well as the power to pay from the assets of the trust reasonable fees necessary to administer the trust.

The trust shall terminate when the child reaches the age specified above and the remaining assets distributed to the child, unless they have been exhausted sooner. In the event the child dies prior to the termination of the trust, then the assets shall pass to the estate of the child. The interests of the beneficiary under this trust shall not be assignable and shall be free from the claims of creditors to the full extent allowed by law.

In the event the said trustee is unable or unwilling to serve for any reason, then I nominate, constitute, and appoint ________________________________ as alternate trustee. No bond shall be required of either trustee in any jurisdiction and this trust shall be administered without court supervision as allowed by law.

SIXTH: In the event any of my children have not attained the age of 18 years at the time of my death, I hereby nominate, constitute, and appoint ________________________________ as guardian over the property of any of my children who have not reached the age of majority at the time of my death. In the event that said guardian is unable or unwilling to serve, then I nominate, constitute, and appoint ________________________________ as guardian. Said guardian shall serve without bond or surety.

SEVENTH: I hereby nominate, constitute, and appoint ________________________ as Personal Representative of this, my Last Will and Testament. In the event that such named person is unable or unwilling to serve at any time or for any reason, then I nominate, constitute, and appoint ________________________ as Personal Representative in the place and stead of the person first named herein. It is my will and I direct that my Personal Representative shall not be required to furnish a bond for the faithful performance of his or her duties in any jurisdiction, any provision of law to the contrary notwithstanding, and I give my Personal Representative full power to administer my estate, including the power to settle claims, pay debts, and sell, lease or exchange real and personal property without court order.

IN WITNESS WHEREOF I declare this to be my Last Will and Testament and execute it willingly as my free and voluntary act for the purposes expressed herein and I am of legal age and sound mind and make this under no constraint or undue influence, this _____ day of ________________, ______.

________________________________L.S.

Each of us declares under penalty of perjury under the laws of the State of California that the following is true and correct:

The foregoing instrument was on said date subscribed at the end thereof by ________________________________, the above named Testator who signed, acknowledged, and published in the presence of us and each of us, who thereupon at his/her request, in his/her presence, and in the presence of each other, have hereunto subscribed our names as witnesses thereto. We are of sound mind and proper age to witness a will and understand this to be his/her will, and to the best of our knowledge testator is of legal age to make a will, of sound mind, and under no constraint or undue influence.

________________________________residing at________________________________

________________________________residing at________________________________

Last Will and Testament

I, ______________________________ a resident of ____________________ County, California do hereby make, publish, and declare this to be my Last Will and Testament, hereby revoking any and all Wills and Codicils heretofore made by me.

FIRST: I direct that all my just debts and funeral expenses be paid out of my estate as soon after my death as is practicable.

SECOND: I give, devise, and bequeath the following specific gifts:

____
____
____
____
____
____
____
____
____
____

THIRD: I give, devise, and bequeath all my estate, real, personal, and mixed, of whatever kind and wherever situated, of which I may die seized or possessed, or in which I may have any interest or over which I may have any power of appointment or testamentary disposition, to my children ____
____
____,
in equal shares, or their lineal descendants per stirpes.

FOURTH: In the event that any beneficiary fails to survive me by thirty days, then this will shall take effect as if that person had predeceased me.

FIFTH: Should my spouse not survive me, I hereby nominate, constitute, and appoint ______________________________ as guardian over the person and estate of any of my children who have not reached the age of majority at the time of my death. In the event that said guardian is unable or unwilling to serve, then I nominate, constitute, and appoint ______________________________ as guardian. Said guardian shall serve without bond or surety.

SIXTH: I hereby nominate, constitute, and appoint ______________________________ as Personal Representative of this, my Last Will and Testament. In the event that such named person is unable or unwilling to serve at any time or for any reason, then I nominate, constitute, and appoint ______________________________ as Personal Representative in the place and stead of the person first named herein. It is my will and I direct that my Personal Representative shall not be required to furnish a bond for the faithful performance of his or her duties in any jurisdiction, any

provision of law to the contrary notwithstanding, and I give my Personal Representative full power to administer my estate, including the power to settle claims, pay debts, and sell, lease or exchange real and personal property without court order.

IN WITNESS WHEREOF I declare this to be my Last Will and Testament and execute it willingly as my free and voluntary act for the purposes expressed herein and I am of legal age and sound mind and make this under no constraint or undue influence, this _____ day of __________________, ______.

_____________________________________L.S.

Each of us declares under penalty of perjury under the laws of the State of California that the following is true and correct:

The foregoing instrument was on said date subscribed at the end thereof by ____, the above named Testator who signed, acknowledged, and published in the presence of us and each of us, who thereupon at his/her request, in his/her presence, and in the presence of each other, have hereunto subscribed our names as witnesses thereto. We are of sound mind and proper age to witness a will and understand this to be his/her will, and to the best of our knowledge testator is of legal age to make a will, of sound mind, and under no constraint or undue influence.

____residing at_____________________________________

____residing at_____________________________________

Last Will and Testament

I, ______________________________________ a resident of ______________________ County, California do hereby make, publish, and declare this to be my Last Will and Testament, hereby revoking any and all Wills and Codicils heretofore made by me.

FIRST: I direct that all my just debts and funeral expenses be paid out of my estate as soon after my death as is practicable.

SECOND: I give, devise, and bequeath the following specific gifts:

____
____
____
____
____
____
____
____
____
____

THIRD: I give, devise, and bequeath all my estate, real, personal, and mixed, of whatever kind and wherever situated, of which I may die seized or possessed, or in which I may have any interest or over which I may have any power of appointment or testamentary disposition, to my children ____
____
____, in equal shares, or their lineal descendants per capita.

FOURTH: In the event that any beneficiary fails to survive me by thirty days, then this will shall take effect as if that person had predeceased me.

FIFTH: Should my spouse not survive me, I hereby nominate, constitute, and appoint ____________________________________ as guardian over the person and estate of any of my children who have not reached the age of majority at the time of my death. In the event that said guardian is unable or unwilling to serve, then I nominate, constitute, and appoint ____________________________________ as guardian. Said guardian shall serve without bond or surety.

SIXTH: I hereby nominate, constitute, and appoint ____________________________ as Personal Representative of this, my Last Will and Testament. In the event that such named person is unable or unwilling to serve at any time or for any reason, then I nominate, constitute, and appoint ______________________________ as Personal Representative in the place and stead of the person first named herein. It is my will and I direct that my Personal Representative shall not be required to furnish a bond for the faithful performance of his or her duties in any jurisdiction, any

provision of law to the contrary notwithstanding, and I give my Personal Representative full power to administer my estate, including the power to settle claims, pay debts, and sell, lease or exchange real and personal property without court order.

IN WITNESS WHEREOF I declare this to be my Last Will and Testament and execute it willingly as my free and voluntary act for the purposes expressed herein and I am of legal age and sound mind and make this under no constraint or undue influence, this _____ day of __________________, ______.

______________________________________L.S.

Each of us declares under penalty of perjury under the laws of the State of California that the following is true and correct:

The foregoing instrument was on said date subscribed at the end thereof by ______________________________________, the above named Testator who signed, acknowledged, and published in the presence of us and each of us, who thereupon at his/her request, in his/her presence, and in the presence of each other, have hereunto subscribed our names as witnesses thereto. We are of sound mind and proper age to witness a will and understand this to be his/her will, and to the best of our knowledge testator is of legal age to make a will, of sound mind, and under no constraint or undue influence.

______________________________________residing at______________________________________

______________________________________residing at______________________________________

Last Will and Testament

I, ______________________________________ a resident of ______________________ County, California do hereby make, publish, and declare this to be my Last Will and Testament, hereby revoking any and all Wills and Codicils heretofore made by me.

FIRST: I direct that all my just debts and funeral expenses be paid out of my estate as soon after my death as is practicable.

SECOND: I give, devise, and bequeath the following specific gifts:

____

____

____

____

____

____

____

____

____

____

THIRD: I give, devise, and bequeath all my estate, real, personal, and mixed, of whatever kind and wherever situated, of which I may die seized or possessed, or in which I may have any interest or over which I may have any power of appointment or testamentary disposition, to the following:____

____

____,

or to the survivor of them.

FOURTH: In the event that any beneficiary fails to survive me by thirty days, then this will shall take effect as if that person had predeceased me.

FIFTH: I hereby nominate, constitute, and appoint ______________________________ as Personal Representative of this, my Last Will and Testament. In the event that such named person is unable or unwilling to serve at any time or for any reason, then I nominate, constitute, and appoint ________________________________ as Personal Representative in the place and stead of the person first named herein. It is my will and I direct that my Personal Representative shall not be required to furnish a bond for the faithful performance of his or her duties in any jurisdiction, any provision of law to the contrary notwithstanding, and I give my Personal Representative full power to administer my estate, including the power to settle claims, pay debts, and sell, lease or exchange real and personal property without court order.

IN WITNESS WHEREOF I declare this to be my Last Will and Testament and execute it willingly as my free and voluntary act for the purposes expressed herein and I am of legal age and

sound mind and make this under no constraint or undue influence, this _____ day of __________________, ______.

__________________________________L.S.

Each of us declares under penalty of perjury under the laws of the State of California that the following is true and correct:

The foregoing instrument was on said date subscribed at the end thereof by ______________________________________, the above named Testator who signed, acknowledged, and published in the presence of us and each of us, who thereupon at his/her request, in his/her presence, and in the presence of each other, have hereunto subscribed our names as witnesses thereto. We are of sound mind and proper age to witness a will and understand this to be his/her will, and to the best of our knowledge testator is of legal age to make a will, of sound mind, and under no constraint or undue influence.

______________________________________residing at____________________________________

______________________________________residing at____________________________________

Last Will and Testament

I, ______________________________ a resident of ____________________ County, California do hereby make, publish, and declare this to be my Last Will and Testament, hereby revoking any and all Wills and Codicils heretofore made by me.

FIRST: I direct that all my just debts and funeral expenses be paid out of my estate as soon after my death as is practicable.

SECOND: I give, devise, and bequeath the following specific gifts:

____

____

____

____

____

____

____

____

____

____

THIRD: I give, devise, and bequeath all my estate, real, personal, and mixed, of whatever kind and wherever situated, of which I may die seized or possessed, or in which I may have any interest or over which I may have any power of appointment or testamentary disposition, to the following ____

____

____,

in equal shares, or their lineal descendants per stirpes.

FOURTH: In the event that any beneficiary fails to survive me by thirty days, then this will shall take effect as if that person had predeceased me.

FIFTH: I hereby nominate, constitute, and appoint ______________________________ as Personal Representative of this, my Last Will and Testament. In the event that such named person is unable or unwilling to serve at any time or for any reason, then I nominate, constitute, and appoint ______________________________ as Personal Representative in the place and stead of the person first named herein. It is my will and I direct that my Personal Representative shall not be required to furnish a bond for the faithful performance of his or her duties in any jurisdiction, any provision of law to the contrary notwithstanding, and I give my Personal Representative full power to administer my estate, including the power to settle claims, pay debts, and sell, lease or exchange real and personal property without court order.

IN WITNESS WHEREOF I declare this to be my Last Will and Testament and execute it willingly as my free and voluntary act for the purposes expressed herein and I am of legal age and

sound mind and make this under no constraint or undue influence, this _____ day of _________________, ______.

_______________________________________L.S.

Each of us declares under penalty of perjury under the laws of the State of California that the following is true and correct:

The foregoing instrument was on said date subscribed at the end thereof by _______________________________________, the above named Testator who signed, acknowledged, and published in the presence of us and each of us, who thereupon at his/her request, in his/her presence, and in the presence of each other, have hereunto subscribed our names as witnesses thereto. We are of sound mind and proper age to witness a will and understand this to be his/her will, and to the best of our knowledge testator is of legal age to make a will, of sound mind, and under no constraint or undue influence.

_______________________________________residing at_____________________________________

_______________________________________residing at_____________________________________

Codicil to the Will of

____

I, ______________________________________, a resident of _____________________ County, California declare this to be the first codicil to my Last Will and Testament dated _____________________, ______.

FIRST: I hereby revoke the clause of my Will which reads as follows: ____
____
____
____.

SECOND: I hereby add the following clause to my Will: ____________________________
____
____
____
____.

THIRD: In all other respects I hereby confirm and republish my Last Will and Testament dated _____________________, ________.

IN WITNESS WHEREOF, I have signed, published, and declared the foregoing instrument as and for a codicil to my Last Will and Testament, this ___________ day of _____________________, _______.

____

The foregoing instrument was on the _________day of __________________, ______, signed at the end thereof, and at the same time published and declared by _________________________________, as and for a codicil to his/her Last Will and Testament, dated ______________________, ________, in the presence of each of us, who, this attestation clause having been read to us, did at the request of the said testator/testatrix, in his/her presence and in the presence of each other signed our names as witnesses thereto.

______________________________residing at______________________________________

______________________________residing at______________________________________

Living Will

Declaration made this _______ day of ____________________, ________.

I, ____, willfully and voluntarily make known that my life not be artificially prolonged under the circumstances set forth below.

If at any time I have a terminal condition and if my attending or treating physician and another consulting physician have determined that there can be no medical probability of my recovery from such condition, I direct my attending physician, pursuant to the Natural Death Act of California, to withhold or withdraw life-prolonging procedures when the application of such procedures would serve only to prolong artificially the process of dying, and that I be permitted to die naturally.

In the absence of my ability to give directions on the use of such life-prolonging procedures, it is my intention that this declaration be honored by my family and physician as the final expression of my legal right to refuse medical or surgical treatment and to accept the consequences for such refusal.

If I have been diagnosed as pregnant, and that diagnosis is known to my physician, this declaration shall have no force or effect during my pregnancy.

I understand the full import of this declaration, and am emotionally and mentally competent to make this declaration.

Additional Instructions (optional):

____

____

____

____

Signature

____

Address

____

The declarant voluntarily signed this writing in my presence. I am not entitled to any portion of the declarant's estate upon his or her death. I am not a health care provider, the operator of a community care facility, the operator of a residential care facility for the elderly or an employee of any of the above.

____

Witness

____

____

Address

The declarant voluntarily signed this writing in my presence. I am not entitled to any portion of the declarant's estate upon his or her death. I am not a health care provider, the operator of a community care facility, the operator of a residential care facility for the elderly or an employee of any of the above.

____

Witness

____

____

Address

UNIFORM DONOR CARD

The undersigned hereby makes this anatomical gift, if medically acceptable, to take effect on death. The words and marks below indicate my desires:

I give:

(a) ____ any needed organs or parts;

(b) ____ only the following organs or parts

____

for the purpose of transplantation, therapy, medical research, or education;

(c) ____ my body for anatomical study if needed.

Limitations or special wishes, if any:

____

Signed by the donor and the following witnesses in the presence of each other:

Signature of Donor	Date of birth
Date signed	City & State
Witness	Witness
Address	Address

UNIFORM DONOR CARD

The undersigned hereby makes this anatomical gift, if medically acceptable, to take effect on death. The words and marks below indicate my desires:

I give:

(a) ____ any needed organs or parts;

(b) ____ only the following organs or parts

____

for the purpose of transplantation, therapy, medical research, or education;

(c) ____ my body for anatomical study if needed.

Limitations or special wishes, if any:

____

Signed by the donor and the following witnesses in the presence of each other:

Signature of Donor	Date of birth
Date signed	City & State
Witness	Witness
Address	Address

UNIFORM DONOR CARD

The undersigned hereby makes this anatomical gift, if medically acceptable, to take effect on death. The words and marks below indicate my desires:

I give:

(a) ____ any needed organs or parts;

(b) ____ only the following organs or parts

____

for the purpose of transplantation, therapy, medical research, or education;

(c) ____ my body for anatomical study if needed.

Limitations or special wishes, if any:

____

Signed by the donor and the following witnesses in the presence of each other:

Signature of Donor	Date of birth
Date signed	City & State
Witness	Witness
Address	Address

UNIFORM DONOR CARD

The undersigned hereby makes this anatomical gift, if medically acceptable, to take effect on death. The words and marks below indicate my desires:

I give:

(a) ____ any needed organs or parts;

(b) ____ only the following organs or parts

____

for the purpose of transplantation, therapy, medical research, or education;

(c) ____ my body for anatomical study if needed.

Limitations or special wishes, if any:

____

Signed by the donor and the following witnesses in the presence of each other:

Signature of Donor	Date of birth
Date signed	City & State
Witness	Witness
Address	Address

One of these cards should be cut out and carried in your wallet or purse.

INDEX

A

B

C

D

E

F

G

H

I

J

Your #1 Source for Real World Legal Information...

SPHINX® PUBLISHING

A Division of Sourcebooks, Inc.®

- Written by lawyers
- Simple English explanation of the law
- Forms and instructions included

HOW TO FILE FOR DIVORCE IN CALIFORNIA

This book provides a step-by-step guide for obtaining a divorce in California without a lawyer. Learn about alimony; child support, custody and visitation; property division; simplified procedures; emergency procedures and more.

208 pages; $19.95;
ISBN 1-57071-355-3

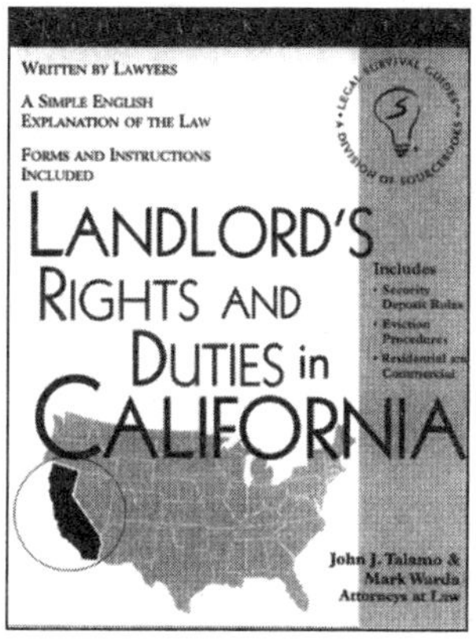

LANDLORDS' RIGHTS & DUTIES IN CALIFORNIA

Covering the law for residential and commercial landlords, from tenant applications to evictions, this book will help California landlords avoid legal problems. Includes California statutes; flowcharts; sample and blank forms.

240 pages; $19.95;
ISBN 1-57071-359-6

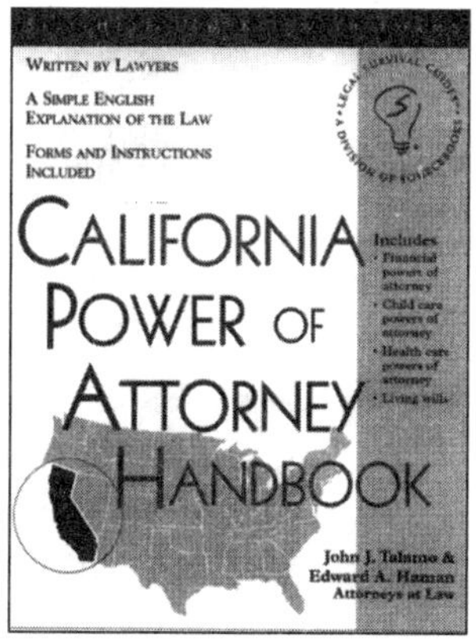

CALIFORNIA POWER OF ATTORNEY HANDBOOK

Now it is easier than ever to authorize someone to act on your behalf for your convenience or necessity. With forms and instructions, this book allows you to draft your own power of attorney for financial matters, health care, real estate and child care.

128 pages; $12.95;
ISBN 1-57071-360-X

OTHER CALIFORNIA LEGAL SURVIVAL GUIDES

How to Win in Small Claims Court in CA	$14.95
How to Probate an Estate in CA	$19.95
How to Start a Business in CA	$16.95

SEE OUR ORDER FORM FOR BOOKS WRITTEN FOR OTHER STATES. COMING SOON: OHIO!

WHAT OUR CUSTOMERS SAY ABOUT OUR BOOKS:

"Your real estate contracts book has saved me nearly $12,000.00 in closing costs over the past year." —A.B.

"...many of the legal questions that I have had over the years were answered clearly and concisely through your plain English interpretation of the law." —C.E.H.

"If there weren't people out there like you I'd be lost. You have the best books of this type out there." —S.B

Legal Survival Guides are directly available from Sourcebooks, Inc., or from your local bookstores.
For credit card orders call 1–800–43–BRIGHT, write P.O. Box 372, Naperville, IL 60566, or fax 630-961-2168

Sphinx® Publishing's National Titles

Valid in All 50 States

Legal Survival in Business

How to Form Your Own Corporation (2E)	$19.95
How to Form Your Own Partnership	$19.95
How to Register Your Own Copyright (2E)	$19.95
How to Register Your Own Trademark (2E)	$19.95
Most Valuable Business Legal Forms You'll Ever Need (2E)	$19.95
Most Valuable Corporate Forms You'll Ever Need (2E)	$24.95
Software Law (with diskette)	$29.95

Legal Survival in Court

Crime Victim's Guide to Justice	$19.95
Debtors' Rights (3E)	$12.95
Defend Yourself Against Criminal Charges	$19.95
Grandparents' Rights	$19.95
Help Your Lawyer Win Your Case	$12.95
Jurors' Rights (2E)	$9.95
Legal Malpractice and Other Claims Against Your Lawyer	$18.95
Legal Research Made Easy (2E)	$14.95
Simple Ways to Protect Yourself From Lawsuits	$24.95
Victims' Rights	$12.95
Winning Your Personal Injury Claim	$19.95

Legal Survival in Real Estate

How to Buy a Condominium or Townhome	$16.95
How to Negotiate Real Estate Contracts (3E)	$16.95
How to Negotiate Real Estate Leases (3E)	$16.95
Successful Real Estate Brokerage Management	$19.95

Legal Survival in Personal Affairs

How to File Your Own Bankruptcy (4E)	$19.95
How to File Your Own Divorce (3E)	$19.95
How to Make Your Own Will	$12.95
How to Write Your Own Living Will	$9.95
How to Write Your Own Premarital Agreement (2E)	$19.95
How to Win Your Unemployment Compensation Claim	$19.95
Living Trusts and Simple Ways to Avoid Probate (2E)	$19.95
Most Valuable Personal Legal Forms You'll Ever Need	$14.95
Neighbor vs. Neighbor	$12.95
The Power of Attorney Handbook (3E)	$19.95
Simple Ways to Protect Yourself from Lawsuits	$24.95
Social Security Benefits Handbook (2E)	$14.95
Unmarried Parents' Rights	$19.95
U.S.A. Immigration Guide (3E)	$19.95
Guia de Inmigracion a Estados Unidos	$19.95

Legal Survival Guides are directly available from Sourcebooks, Inc., or from your local bookstores.

For credit card orders call 1–800–43–BRIGHT, write P.O. Box 372, Naperville, IL 60566, or fax 630-961-2168

SPHINX® PUBLISHING ORDER FORM

BILL TO:		SHIP TO:	
Phone #	Terms	F.O.B. Chicago, IL	Ship Date

Charge my: ❒ VISA ❒ MasterCard ❒ American Express

❒ **Money Order or Personal Check**

Credit Card Number ____________ Expiration Date ____

Qty	ISBN	Title	Retail	Ext.
		SPHINX PUBLISHING NATIONAL TITLES		
____	1-57071-166-6	Crime Victim's Guide to Justice	$19.95	____
____	1-57071-342-1	Debtors' Rights (3E)	$12.95	____
____	1-57071-162-3	Defend Yourself Against Criminal Charges	$19.95	____
____	1-57248-001-7	Grandparents' Rights	$19.95	____
____	0-913825-99-9	Guia de Inmigracion a Estados Unidos	$19.95	____
____	1-57248-021-1	Help Your Lawyer Win Your Case	$12.95	____
____	1-57071-164-X	How to Buy a Condominium or Townhome	$16.95	____
____	1-57071-223-9	How to File Your Own Bankruptcy (4E)	$19.95	____
____	1-57071-224-7	How to File Your Own Divorce (3E)	$19.95	____
____	1-57071-227-1	How to Form Your Own Corporation (2E)	$19.95	____
____	1-57071-343-X	How to Form Your Own Partnership	$19.95	____
____	1-57071-228-X	How to Make Your Own Will	$12.95	____
____	1-57071-331-6	How to Negotiate Real Estate Contracts (3E)	$16.95	____
____	1-57071-332-4	How to Negotiate Real Estate Leases (3E)	$16.95	____
____	1-57071-225-5	How to Register Your Own Copyright (2E)	$19.95	____
____	1-57071-226-3	How to Register Your Own Trademark (2E)	$19.95	____
____	1-57071-349-9	How to Win Your Unemployment Compensation Claim	$19.95	____
____	1-57071-167-4	How to Write Your Own Living Will	$9.95	____
____	1-57071-344-8	How to Write Your Own Premarital Agreement (2E)	$19.95	____
____	1-57071-333-2	Jurors' Rights (2E)	$9.95	____
____	1-57248-032-7	Legal Malpractice and Other Claims Against...	$18.95	____
____	1-57071-400-2	Legal Research Made Easy (2E)	$14.95	____
____	1-57071-336-7	Living Trusts and Simple Ways to Avoid Probate (2E)	$19.95	____
____	1-57071-345-6	Most Valuable Bus. Legal Forms You'll Ever Need (2E)	$19.95	____
____	1-57071-346-4	Most Valuable Corporate Forms You'll Ever Need (2E)	$24.95	____
____	1-57071-347-2	Most Valuable Personal Legal Forms You'll Ever Need	$14.95	____
____	0-913825-41-7	Neighbor vs. Neighbor	$12.95	____
____	1-57071-348-0	The Power of Attorney Handbook (3E)	$19.95	____
____	1-57248-020-3	Simple Ways to Protect Yourself from Lawsuits	$24.95	____
____	1-57071-337-5	Social Security Benefits Handbook (2E)	$14.95	____
____	1-57071-163-1	Software Law (w/diskette)	$29.95	____
____	0-913825-86-7	Successful Real Estate Brokerage Mgmt.	$19.95	____
____	1-57071-399-5	Unmarried Parents' Rights	$19.95	____
____	1-57071-354-5	U.S.A. Immigration Guide (3E)	$19.95	____
____	0-913825-82-4	Victims' Rights	$12.95	____
____	1-57071-165-8	Winning Your Personal Injury Claim	$19.95	____
		CALIFORNIA TITLES		
____	1-57071-360-X	CA Power of Attorney Handbook	$12.95	____
____	1-57071-355-3	How to File for Divorce in CA	$19.95	____
____	1-57071-356-1	How to Make a CA Will	$12.95	____
____	1-57071-408-8	How to Probate an Estate in CA	$19.95	____
____	1-57071-357-X	How to Start a Business in CA	$16.95	____
____	1-57071-358-8	How to Win in Small Claims Court in CA	$14.95	____
____	1-57071-359-6	Landlords' Rights and Duties in CA	$19.95	____
		FLORIDA TITLES		
____	1-57071-363-4	Florida Power of Attorney Handbook (2E)	$9.95	____
____	1-57071-403-7	How to File for Divorce in FL (5E)	$21.95	____
____	1-57071-401-0	How to Form a Partnership in FL	$19.95	____
____	1-57248-004-1	How to Form a Nonprofit Corp. in FL (3E)	$19.95	____
____	1-57071-380-4	How to Form a Corporation in FL (4E)	$19.95	____
____	1-57071-361-8	How to Make a FL Will (5E)	$12.95	____

____ ***Form Continued on Following Page*** **SUBTOTAL** ____

To order, call Sourcebooks at 1-800-43-BRIGHT or FAX (630)961-2168 (Bookstores, libraries, wholesalers—please call for discount)

SPHINX® PUBLISHING ORDER FORM

Qty	ISBN	Title	Retail	Ext.
		FLORIDA TITLES (CONT'D)		
____	1-57248-056-4	How to Modify Your FL Divorce Judgement (3E)	$22.95	____
____	1-57071-364-2	How to Probate an Estate in FL (3E)	$24.95	____
____	1-57248-005-X	How to Start a Business in FL (4E)	$16.95	____
____	1-57071-362-6	How to Win in Small Claims Court in FL (6E)	$14.95	____
____	1-57071-335-9	Landlords' Rights and Duties in FL (7E)	$19.95	____
____	1-57071-334-0	Land Trusts in FL (5E)	$24.95	____
____	0-913825-73-5	Women's Legal Rights in FL	$19.95	____
		GEORGIA TITLES		
____	1-57071-387-1	How to File for Divorce in GA (3E)	$19.95	____
____	1-57248-047-5	How to Make a GA Will (2E)	$9.95	____
____	1-57248-026-2	How to Start and Run a GA Business (2E)	$18.95	____
		ILLINOIS TITLES		
____	1-57071-405-3	How to File for Divorce in IL (2E)	$19.95	____
____	1-57071-415-0	How to Make an IL Will (2E)	$12.95	____
____	1-57071-416-9	How to Start a Business in IL (2E)	$16.95	____
		MASSACHUSETTS TITLES		
____	1-57071-329-4	How to File for Divorce in MA (2E)	$19.95	____
____	1-57248-050-5	How to Make a MA Will	$9.95	____
____	1-57248-053-X	How to Probate an Estate in MA	$19.95	____
____	1-57248-054-8	How to Start a Business in MA	$16.95	____
____	1-57248-055-6	Landlords' Rights and Duties in MA	$19.95	____
		MICHIGAN TITLES		
____	1-57071-409-6	How to File for Divorce in MI (2E)	$19.95	____
____	1-57248-015-7	How to Make a MI Will	$9.95	____
____	1-57071-407-X	How to Start a Business in MI (2E)	$16.95	____
		MINNESOTA TITLES		
____	1-57248-039-4	How to File for Divorce in MN	$19.95	____
____	1-57248-040-8	How to Form a Simple Corporation in MN	$19.95	____
____	1-57248-037-8	How to Make a MN Will	$9.95	____
____	1-57248-038-6	How to Start a Business in MN	$16.95	____

Qty	ISBN	Title	Retail	Ext.
		NEW YORK TITLES		
____	1-57071-184-4	How to File for Divorce in NY	$19.95	____
____	1-57071-183-6	How to Make a NY Will	$12.95	____
____	1-57071-185-2	How to Start a Business in NY	$16.95	____
____	1-57071-187-9	How to Win in Small Claims Court in NY	$14.95	____
____	1-57071-186-0	Landlords' Rights and Duties in NY	$19.95	____
____	1-57071-188-7	New York Power of Attorney Handbook	$19.95	____
		NORTH CAROLINA TITLES		
____	1-57071-326-X	How to File for Divorce in NC (2E)	$19.95	____
____	1-57071-327-8	How to Make a NC Will (2E)	$12.95	____
____	0-913825-93-X	How to Start a Business in NC	$16.95	____
		PENNSYLVANIA TITLES		
____	1-57071-177-1	How to File for Divorce in PA	$19.95	____
____	1-57071-176-3	How to Make a PA Will	$12.95	____
____	1-57071-178-X	How to Start a Business in PA	$16.95	____
____	1-57071-179-8	Landlords' Rights and Duties in PA	$19.95	____
		TEXAS TITLES		
____	1-57071-330-8	How to File for Divorce in TX (2E)	$19.95	____
____	1-57248-009-2	How to Form a Simple Corporation in TX	$19.95	____
____	1-57071-417-7	How to Make a TX Will (2E)	$12.95	____
____	1-57071-418-5	How to Probate an Estate in TX (2E)	$19.95	____
____	1-57071-365-0	How to Start a Business in TX (2E)	$16.95	____
____	1-57248-012-2	How to Win in Small Claims Court in TX	$14.95	____
____	1-57248-011-4	Landlords' Rights and Duties in TX	$19.95	____

SUBTOTAL THIS PAGE ____

SUBTOTAL PREVIOUS PAGE ____

Illinois residents add 6.75% sales tax
Florida residents add 6% state sales tax plus applicable discretionary surtax ____

Shipping— $4.00 for 1st book, $1.00 each additional ____

TOTAL ____